"LITTLE WAY OF MOTHERHOOD"

By Julie Larsen

A Catholic Walk into Pregnancy and "Little Way of Pregnancy"

Table of Contents:

Letter of Introduction:

Dear Mother or Pregnant mother:

Congratulations in your pregnancy! We hope this book will help you prepare for the arrival of your baby! This book goes through various stages of pregnancy to having a baptism and Woman Churching ceremony. We sprinkle quotes from St. Therese the Little Flower (hey, one of my favorite saints) – thus the name "Little Way of Motherhood" – it could also be titled "Little Way of Pregnancy" and you are becoming a mother and I think it is an appropriate title! There are some crafting and cooking sections in some of this book – called "St. Anne's corner" – hope you enjoy these sections.

Dear Doulas and Dads:

If you are a dad and wanting some tips, this book does include a few dad boot camp sections, make sure to read those little extra sections to learn more about being a father and helping your wife prepare for labor!

Doulas – if you happen to be a birth worker picking up this book to read, great! We have a couple of sections sprinkled throughout on how doulas can help moms too!

I hope everyone who reads this book will obtain some new knowledge of mothering or pregnancy!

God bless,

Julie Larsen P.S. Find my book "Comfort in Birth Method" if you need tips on how to have a more natural labor. Thank you.

Find more about my books at www.catholicpostpartum.com

Chapter One: Introduction and how to use this book.

"When I die, I will send down a shower of roses from the heavens, I will spend my heaven by doing good on earth." -St. Therese of Lisieux.[i]

Welcome to the "Little Way of Motherhood." These pages are penned in loving way to share the journey of motherhood with you. We will start at the beginning of your pregnancy and walk you through the weeks of preparation for your little one's arrival. We will be giving you tips and hints on how to help you throughout this book. We started out with biweekly – but at the end we decided to do shorter synopsis of later trimester in order to fit in breastfeeding section.

We want this book to be for dads as well – so we will kind of have this pause or area for dads. It will be titled "Dad Boot camp" in those sections. This way the father of the baby can enjoy a few tips. We also include tips for doulas. I am a doula and I think that it would be nice to have a pregnancy book that is written in a way that doulas can benefit. So, we will have a little section called "Doula Tips" – this will be for the doulas reading the book. It will give you tips on how to support the mom during this time of her pregnancy or ideas on how to help her during labor.

Crafts! Yes, I get creative and feel that sometimes we want more hands-on things to do while pregnant as a mother. If you are reading this as a first-time mom, you will more likely have more time to make a little craft or sewn item for your upcoming birth – so we will give a few things in this book to do – it will be under "St. Anne crafts for moms". Why St. Anne? Well, she's the grandmother of Jesus – so she is a good patroness of helping moms!

Journaling sections: We hope to give you a place to write down your thoughts about your pregnancy and upcoming birth.

There are also various saints "scattered" throughout each section; so we added a short section in the back for extra saints to read about and pray to for pregnancy and miscarriage help. We hope you enjoy this book.

Why the title "Little Way to Motherhood?" St. Therese is not a mother, but she has given us her "Little Way" to heaven which is great for mothers as well as anyone. St. Therese promised to send down a "shower of roses" from heaven; and I want to share little quotes from St. Therese for each of the chapters of this book! We will also talk a little bit more about St. Therese's little way in some of the chapters. If you are not familiar with her "Little Way", we hope to show you this way! We believe that St. Therese can be a saint of motherhood as well!

<u>Journaling space:</u>

<u>**Chapter 2 – First weeks of pregnancy (weeks 1-5)**</u>

St. Therese Quote for this chapter: A mother may feel anxious at the beginning of her pregnancy – here is what St. Therese had to say about anxiety:

"If I did not simply live from one moment to another, it would be impossible for me to be patient; but I only look at the present, I forget the past, and I take good care not to forestall the future."[ii]

"What are pregnancy symptoms – to "finding out".

You are most likely not going to know you are pregnant right away. You will go through your day as normal. So, you are most likely not going to find out till week 5 or week 6 of pregnancy though some moms find out during week 4 – rarely any sooner.

So, how do you know if you are pregnant? What are the symptoms? Well, my mother-in-law always knew as she would throw up – some mothers feel really bad when they first become pregnant. Myself, I usually just more or less had some nausea – but this really seem to set in more after I "found out" that I was pregnant. Sometimes one doesn't really have that many symptoms. Also, your breasts maybe sorer esp. if this is a second pregnancy – and you might still be nursing still – then you may notice this more. You may also notice milk coming out of your breasts (first or subsequent pregnancy). Here's a meditation section:

Commentary on pre-pregnancy or conception

The first two weeks of any pregnancy is usually pre-pregnancy since the doctors start with your last known menstrual cycle. Or your baby might be just forming but so tiny that there would most likely not be a positive pregnancy test yet. Your baby is conceived after the sperm meets the egg and traveling up the fallopian tube to the new home in the uterus.

If you are like me, I dread the first few days of my cycle. I sometimes have bad headaches as result of the cycle. I can sympathize with anyone who is not able to do much during their "time of the month". You maybe just finishing and thinking your husband is wanting you. What if you feel like you are not ready for pregnancy yet? We are not going to talk about *contraception* or *birth control* in this book since we are Catholic and believe in follow God's plan for a family.

Communicating is important in marriage and you should communicate with your husband. It is important to communicate your feelings to your husband about your cycles and such. If he's a good husband, he will listen to you and validate your feelings of fear or whatever issues you might be concerned about.

What if you are ready and he's not? Then, try to wait and take your time conceiving your first or subsequent child. God has His Own timing as far as conception goes. Sometimes a mother may find it easy to conceive and other times not so easy if it is God's will then the child will be conceived. If not, then it is not God's will. Waiting a little longer might be what God has called you to do. If you are "surprised" at a pregnancy, do not fear God is with you in this time. A lot of mothers esp. if this is their first pregnancy – they may have had plans to continue their "career" outside the home when a pregnancy comes. Perhaps, God is telling this mother to slow down and let her husband to take over. The traditional family ways have been the husband being the "breadwinner" of the family. However, these days we know that sometimes both parents have to work. It may be a sacrifice, but sometimes it is best for the mother to stop working and let the husband take over. Our meditation here is to consider – What is God's will for me now that I am pregnant as a mother? Am I scared or afraid? We will be going over an exercise about fear in this section too. Also, it is God's will for me to stop a career if I have one? If keeping my career, how will I juggle family life and work?

Were you ever surprised in a pregnancy? Is this a surprise pregnancy? Are you afraid? What pregnancy is this for you? Have you shared your pregnancy with your friends yet? Journal a few thought about this here:

____

____

____

Mary Meditation: "Walking with Mary: Mary's Birth"

Our Lady had to be born before she could be the Mother of us all. St. Anne was Mary's Mother. St. Anne was considered "barren" as she was an older mother. She was quite surprised to become pregnant in her old age. It seems that she might have had an inclination that this child was to be special. Imagine the Immaculate Conception of Mary—Mary was conceived without sin inside of St. Anne's Womb. St. Anne's birth of Mary was probably painless as she was the mother of the Mother of God. It must have been a special birth with angels surrounding the Blessed Virgin Mary at her birth. Another thing to consider is this was God's will for Mary to be conceived without sin; but ultimately her decision to be God's mother. However, who could say "no" to a request from the angel – and God saying to Mary through the angel Gabriel – that this will happen? Mary's "Fiat", yes to God started at her conception! Mary's yes to God continued through her birth and throughout her life. Remember to embrace Mary's title of "O Mary Conceived Without Sin, Pray for us who recourse to thee." She gave us this title to St. Catherine Labore' and also the title "I am the Immaculate Conception," was also given to us through St. Bernadette. So, God wanted us to have both of these great saints to get HIS will across that Mary should be addressed by this title. Also, God allowed a special medal called the "Miraculous Medal" to be used to help convert others. The original title of this medal was the "Immaculate conception medal." I found out recently that you can now be enrolled in the Miraculous Medal if you go to a priest that does the Latin Tridentine Mass or "Extraordinary Form" – he will have the right prayers to enroll you in this medal.

Meditate on this scene for a few minutes.

Prayer Request: "O, St. Anne mother of the Mother of God, please pray for us that we will come to knowledge of Mary's Immaculate Conception and to understand this mystery better. O, St. Anne, I also pray for God's will on conceiving a child or carrying this child already conceived to full-term if God's will. Amen."

You may want to journal about St. Anne as mother of Mary:

____

____

____

____

____

____

<u>Dad-Boot Camp Tips: Finding out story:</u>

"When my wife first found out she was pregnant during our very first pregnancy, I thought she was so cute. She had gotten up to pee and take the test. Then she came to me and said – 'I think I am pregnant.' Those few words gave me the weirdest feeling in my whole life – it was like this great sensation – I couldn't believe it – I am going to be a dad! I wanted to look at the test – yes it was positive. I wanted to re-test – so we did the following day – yep, positive again! So, we found a midwife to contact. We had already discussed if my wife had ever gotten pregnant, we would hire a midwife since they are more natural for birth and all. We found a midwife up the road from our house. She came over and we did a test for her and first intake forms about a month after we found out. We were super excited to work with this midwife." – _Anonymous dad._

For Dads Tip #1: Always support your wife when she wants to do something special about her pregnancy/upcoming birth. Let's say she wants to go on a small trip to see her mother. Let her do so. She may be feeling more sentimental right now. Write one way you will support your wife during this pregnancy:

____

____

____

Mom Tip #1 – Always include dad in "finding out" that you are pregnant – maybe surprise him in a special way. One of my pregnancies, I had made a card for him – he had gone off to school that morning and when he got back - he had this "early" Father's day card waiting for him – inside the card was a picture of a "stork". He really liked that! Write down a way you will surprise dad or a way you surprised him in the past:

____.

St. Anne's Corner: Announcement Card - Craft Section:

To make a special "finding out card" for your husband or another family member – perhaps you want to send an announcement to your mother or whoever that you are expecting – this little craft idea can be fun to make; you can look on the Internet for a picture of a stork if you like.

Use cardstock or some thicker card style and fold it into a card size (can be in half or fourths depending on what size you like). Then you will trace your stork on to some craft paper (pick a color you like- blue, pink, neutral – this is way too early for gender reveal) then cut out your stork! You can decide whether you want the stork inside the card or outside in front of card. Glue your stork to your card. Now use the other craft decorations – balloons or ribbons (see appendix) and cut out those shapes and add to front of card. Add your own words to the card. The stork should be carrying a baby – if need be, cut the baby out separate and add to the card and you are finished with your "announcement" for pregnancy. If you feel like sharing your crafts – go to our special website or blog to share (add later on in).

Letting Go of Fears Section: (For Both Parents):

Instead of a saint for *this chapter*– we are going to post a short **"letting go of fears of pregnancy"** exercise for mothers to try. Also, dads can do as well. Men can be just as scared about birth!

First of all, sit in and relax in a chair – you may want a friend to work with you on this (or your husband).

Second, write down your fears that you may be experiencing.

Third, think of something that may help battle your fears – a prayer for instance, "Jesus I trust in You". An affirmation, "I am in charge and God has given me this blessing."

Fourth, now tear up or burn your fears that you wrote down – as you tear up or watch them burn – say to yourself – "I let go of these fears."

Fifth – continue saying your prayer above or affirmations that will help you. Now, get up and go about your day! Remember also that we should "yield to God's love." If you feel that fear is filling up your heart; turn to God in prayer at that very moment and ask HIM to take that fear. We may talk a little more later about "yielding to God."

Christ CALM Method – this is based on something I teach in "Comfort in Birth Method" book. C is for Christ, A is for Allow, L is for Let Go and M for Meditation and Motherhood.

The mother can sit quietly in a chair and pray and think about these words/letters:

C = Christ – Who is Jesus Christ to you in your life? And His Mother Mary?

A = Allow – Allow Jesus to Enter – Allow Him to Heal. Allow Him to Help!

L = Let Go – Let go of the tension, Let go of the fears, Let go of whatever is in the way.

M = Meditation/Motherhood – Mary is our Mother and she will help us in meditation and Motherhood – that is what you are becoming a mother (if first time mom) or you may already be a mother and embracing it again with your (second, third, fourth, fifth, sixth, etc. pregnancy!) We congratulate your journey deeper into mothering more! Use the extra journaling space below to write your thoughts about this meditation:

<u>Chapter Three – Weeks 6 and 7:</u>

<u>"Let us love, since that is what our hearts were made for." – St Therese of Lisieux[iii]</u>

As you now have found out for sure you are pregnant, remember to offer love to

the baby inside of you daily!

This is the time when you will probably start to feel a bit nauseated to even vomiting. You just discovered you are now pregnant and are feeling sick. "How can this little bean – make you so ill?" Part of it is hormonal reasons and the other part is that this is partly a foreign substance in a way – the sperm comes in and unites with the egg at conception and now the baby is settling up in the uterus about around 6-7 weeks. So, the body is not use to this – so your body reacts in the most natural way – feeling ill, nausea, sore breasts, vomiting, etc. Motherhood would be nicer if it felt better!

We titled this book **<u>"The Little Way to Motherhood"</u>** in imitation of St. Therese the Little Flower. She was never a real mother; but she found her vocation in helping and praying for priests. Let us consider this a bit.

St. Therese was almost fifteen and her father took her on a trip to Paris and Rome. When they were traveling, they met quite a few priests on their travels. When they stopped the priests would also go with them to the place to stay, etc. At this time St. Therese had regarded priests as high honored men and did not see their faults. However, stopping and going so much with the priests – Therese happened to overhear conversations that perhaps she should not have. This made her see priests as they are – fallen men. She realized then that they needed prayers more than anyone else. For probably less people pray for priests then they should! Therese was honored with having love for these priests and praying for them.

So, why am I talking about praying for priests? Well, as pregnant mothers feeling sick and all – we can offer up our first trimester blues of nausea and discomfort for our local parish priests or any priest that has touched our lives. We can do a decade each day for the priest in mind or a few "Hail Mary's". So, this is something I suggest you try for your favorite priest.

Prayer or Meditation: "Mary come and walk with me and with my parish priest______(name) and please bless him in his vocation to help families and bless his vocation as a priest of God. May he do Your will, and also may he be able to baptize my little one when the time comes. Amen."

Doula Tip Section: Mothers may not be seeking a doula anytime soon yet; but a doula is there to support the whole pregnancy if so desired. If you do start up making as a childbirth educator too, then you may be able to help mothers earlier. Having some nausea helping tips for mothers can be a good thing to offer any mom you come across. There are some natural remedies that can help nausea. Chewing on ginger chews or lozenges with ginger can help mothers. This may help settle a mother's stomach. Another tip is that some mothers may not get enough protein in their diets because of vomiting and such. Having the mother drink a protein shake with protein of her choice, milk or almond milk, and maybe add in some favorite fruit – can help her feel better. I use to do this and I added in peanut butter as it really made it taste great. Just make sure if you are helping a mother early on that she's not allergic to any suggested ingredients. So, next time you hear of a mother with nausea – we hope these two suggestions will help. If you are a mother reading this, you may want to try finding ginger chews and drinking whey protein drinks.

St. Anne's Corner: Recipe time (Creative section); Instead of a craft – we will suggest the following recipe for mothers to eat for protein shake:

One organic banana, 1 scoop of protein shake ingredient (your choice – Jay Robb's whey protein for instance) (Rice Protein if allergic to milk), Almond milk (about one cup) (or Rice Milk if allergic to almonds), 2 Tablespoons of peanut butter (or sunflower butter if allergic to peanuts), Place ingredients into a food shake blender or Ninja and blend well for a minute or two. Put into a cup and mother can enjoy drinking this wonderful mixture.

Journaling space: Write any thoughts about these weeks below:

Chapter 4: Week 8-9 – We hear the heartbeat now!

"The good God does not need years to accomplish His work of love in a soul; one ray from His Heart can, in an instant, make His flower bloom for eternity." – St Therese of Lisieux[iv]

We thought this quote is appropriate for the heartbeat time. Though a heartbeat will most likely not register on a doppler or fetoscope till much later – the child's heart is beating now and sending that little ray's of Love to God!

A mother may go in for her first or second checkup around this time. For me I think it was first checkup. I always did not really find out I was pregnant till around 6 weeks or so. Anyway, you most likely will not pick up a heartbeat on a fetoscope till a little bit later in the pregnancy. However, many mothers get an early ultrasound and that is where you will be able to see and hear the heartbeat of your baby. Even if you are waiting to do an ultrasound till more mid-pregnancy, you can just imagine your baby's little "heart" beating inside of you now. Amazing! You may want to go online and watch a YouTube video of a baby's heartbeat. This is probably also around what we call implantation or maybe a little earlier, the "embryo" will find a place in the mother's uterus to get settled and attach itself to the mother. There might even be light bleeding around this time. This is normal. If you experience any heavy bleeding like a period or more please contact your doctor immediately, there could be something else going on. Let's pray it is not anything like that. We are not covering miscarriages in this book. If you want to read another book about bereavement and such, find the one titled *"Hope Through Sorrow"* that I wrote going through the Seven Sorrows of Mary. Now, that your amazing baby's heart is beating – time for some Catholic meditation!

The Heart of Jesus inside of Mary's Womb! This is a good time to consider the Heart of Jesus as a baby inside Mary's Womb. He was already on fire for the love of us. He wants to come to us as a baby so small and weak. His Love for us to become man and to die for us. Just imagine and think about His 9 months inside of His Mother's Womb. What are your thoughts?

____

____

____

____

O, Sacred Heart of Jesus safe in your mother's Womb, pray for us.

O, Sacred Heart of Jesus, desire of everlasting hills, pray for us.

O, Sacred Heart of Jesus, pray for the babies not safe in their mother's wombs – let us pray those seeking abortion will re-consider life, pray for them.

O, Sacred Heart of Jesus, keep us in Your Heart, pray for us. Amen.

Find the Full Litany of the Sacred Heart of Jesus and pray it once this week!

Dad Boot Camp Section:

Now, that you know you are going to be a father, you may have some questions about babies. If you have taken care of a baby in the past, then you can probably skip this section. Will the baby keep me up all night? Most likely yes or at the beginning. So, what do you do about that? How do you get your sleep, or your wife gets her sleep? First of all, see if you can get some time off of your job/work after the birth. A good 2 weeks would be helpful and a whole month would be ideal. However, we know most employers won't let you off that much in USA. So, talk to the employer and see what you can arrange. If you work for yourself, kudos – you can set your own schedule perhaps hire a part-time temporary helper to do extra work while you help take care of your wife and baby. Also, hiring a postpartum doula maybe helpful. We will talk more about doulas later.

Read the book "The First 40 Days" by Heng Ou together. Postpartum books should be read before having your baby that way you can prepare for all the details ahead of time. Dad if you do not know how to change a diaper, practice on a doll now. Dad if you do not know how to swaddle a baby, then we will give some tips below on that. <u>We think swaddling is important to know so baby will be less fussy, and you can get more sleep.</u> Also, some babies do not like their hands and arms to be tied down- you can do the sleep sack version where they have their hands out if so desired. I also suggest you read the book "Happiest Baby on the

Block" together as you wait for you baby to arrive. Another thing, if you can take a full childbirth class online together, your wife and you will learn so much more than what I can put in this little booklet. I recommend Catholic Doula program's online childbirth class: http://www.catholicdoula.com/parent-classes.html

Write down a class you will attend online:

____.

Remember fathers are usually welcome to attend online class with their wife/partner.

For Dad and Mom: How to swaddle a baby! (For our how-to/crafty section) Moms: First of all you can buy a swaddle or make one. Usually the swaddles online are usually made out of more stretchy fabrics. However, I made kind of baby cozy in the past that tied together (be careful with ties and keep them short). Here's an article you can read online: https://www.healthline.com/health/best-swaddles (Just goes over more of types, etc.) There is the blanket swaddle and then a sack swaddle method.

Below is from Mama Natural website: https://www.mamanatural.com/how-to-swaddle-a-baby/

1. The diamond swaddle

"Lay a blanket down on a safe, flat place for baby in a diamond shape/position with the top-most corner folded down 4-6 inches for baby's head. Lay baby down on their back in the center of the blanket with their neck on the folded corner. Pull the left side over and snugly tuck under baby, making sure to keep baby's hips loose. Never pull their legs straight or force their joints, as this could cause hip dysplasia. Pull the bottom corner up and over baby's left shoulder and then wrap the last corner all the way around baby. Tuck into the little blanket pocket you've created on their front."[v]

Remember to go slow and stay calm. Baby should calm down after being swaddled. Also, if baby keeps putting their arms out, that is **OK**, according to the author of "**The Mommy Plan**", some babies prefer not to have their arms swaddled. You may want to put little mittens on their hands if they have long fingernails! Please see picture below on how to swaddle:

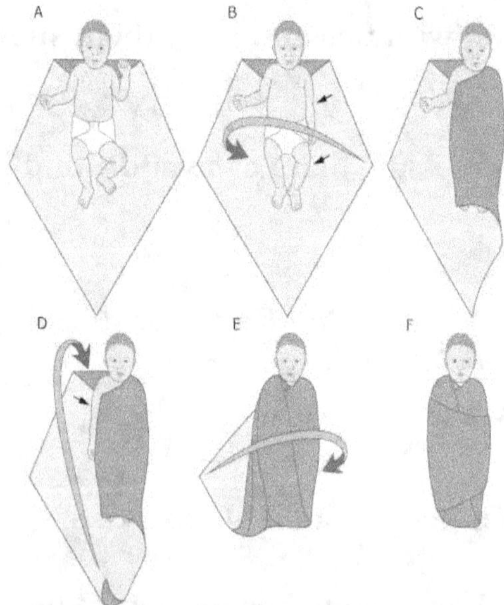

Picture credit[vi] (Diamond Swaddle)

2. Square swaddle or quick swaddle

"If the diamond swaddle isn't for you, don't worry, there are other ways.

Lay a blanket down in a safe, flat place for baby in a square shape/position folding the top right corner down about 4-6 inches for baby's head.

Lay baby down on their back on the blanket with their neck at the top of the fold; baby will be diagonal across the blanket.

Pull the right side over and snugly tuck under baby (always making sure they have frog legs/loose hips).

Pull the left side over, and snugly tuck under baby.

Tuck the bottom of the blanket behind baby and you're good to go."[vii]

Picture credit[viii] This above would be a sleep sack picture with Velcro closing. Note. These may not last as long as Velcro tends to grab "lint" in the washing machines, etc. Also, you may want to cover baby's hands like this picture, so they won't accidentally scratch themselves. They seem to get long fingernails as newborns!

3. Sleep sack swaddle How-to:

"Looking for an even faster option? This method involves a special sleep sack swaddle, but once you've got one it's super simple.

Put baby in sleep sack like you would a onesie or footie pajamas

Zip sleep sack

Wrap and Velcro

These steps will vary depending on which product you purchase and prefer. We will show you some of our favorites later on in this article. Whether you don't have enough time or want the simplicity of not having to wrap baby "just so," a sleep sack is a fine option."[ix]

There are videos in this website if you want to go look at those go to: https://www.mamanatural.com/how-to-swaddle-a-baby/

Now it is your turn – both parents should practice on a doll if you are first time parents. Or if you can find another parent that will allow you to practice on their newborn – that would be great.

How long should a baby stay in a sleep swaddle? Usually around 2-3 months or until the baby starts being more mobile. Like when they want to start crawling around. Some babies may last longer or less time, but this is around the ideal time for swaddling. After that you may want to consider a swing for times you need to be hands free or a jumper for the baby to go in. The baby will be staying awake more. Also, you can consider a baby wrap to carry the baby in.

Saints of Pregnancy Section Part A[x]:

So, far we have talked about St. Anne and St. Therese. Now, it is time to talk about St. Gerard Majella. How did he become known as "the mother's saint?" He is a great patron of pregnancy, so we want to add him in early so you can pray to him throughout your 9 month's time!

Here's why St. Gerard is patroness of mothers – *written by Elizabeth Texeria:*

"Gerard is the unofficial patron saint of mothers and pregnancy. During one of his missionary journeys, as he was leaving the home of friends, one of the family's daughters indicated that he had left his handkerchief behind. Gerard replied, "Keep it. It may come in handy someday." The girl always treasured Gerard's handkerchief. Many years later she was in danger of dying during childbirth. She called for the handkerchief to be brought to her. When she held the handkerchief in her hand, the danger she faced in childbirth disappeared.

On October 15, 1755, Gerard died. Before his death, he had a sign placed on his door that read: "The will of God is done here, as God wills it and as long as He wills it." On December 11, 1904, Gerard was canonized a saint of the Roman Catholic Church."

So, you can see that St. Gerard is highly regarded as a patron of women in labor and childbirth! There are a few websites where you can obtain items of devotion to him.

This website below allows you to enroll in the League of St. Gerard and they send you a nice certificate in the mail at no cost – though donations are gladly accepted: www.themotherssaint.org

Direct link to join the League is here: https://themotherssaint.org/about-the-league/

Obtaining a <u>Hanky of St. Gerard</u> for your pregnancy and upcoming labor maybe something you desire. Here is a link to that via St. Lucy's Church in NJ: https://www.saintlucy.net/st-gerard

Prayer websites: https://www.daily-prayers.org/angels-and-saints/prayers-to-saint-gerard-majella/ and https://www.ourcatholicprayers.com/prayers-to-st-gerard.html

<u>This first prayer to St. Gerard is for Motherhood:</u>

O good St Gerard, powerful intercessor before God and wonder worker of our day, confidently I call upon you and seek your aid. On Earth you always fulfilled God's designs, help me now to do the holy will of God. Implore the Master of Life, from whom all paternity proceeds, to render me fruitful in offspring, that I may raise up children to God in this life, and in the world to come, heirs to the Kingdom of His Glory. Amen.[xi]

<u>Prayer for Safe Delivery (at birth):</u>

O Great Saint Gerard, beloved servant of Jesus Christ, perfect imitator of your meek and humble Savior and devoted child of Mother of God, enkindle within my heart one spark of that heavenly fire of charity which glowed in your heart and made you an angel of love.

O Glorious Saint Gerard, because when falsely accused of a crime, you did bear, like your Divine Master, without murmur or complaint, the calumnies of wicked men, you have been raised up by God as the patron and protector of expectant mothers.

Preserve me from danger and from the excessive pains accompanying childbirth, and shield the child which I now carry, that it may see the light of day and receive the purifying and life-giving waters of baptism through Jesus Christ our Lord. Amen.[xii]

<u>**Prayer Corner: Say some of these prayers daily for a week.**</u>

Meditate on your pregnancy at this time. Journal:

Men should meditate on being like St. Joseph during Mary's pregnancy.

Here is <u>St. Joseph's Prayer for Protection</u>:

Oh, St. Joseph, whose protection is so great, so prompt, so strong, before the throne of God, I place in you all my interests and desires. Oh, St. Joseph, do assist me by your powerful intercession, and obtain for me from your Divine Son all spiritual blessings, through Jesus Christ, our Lord. So that, having engaged here below your heavenly power, I may offer my thanksgiving and homage to the most loving of fathers. Oh, St. Joseph, I never weary contemplating you and Jesus asleep in your arms; I dare not approach while he reposes near your heart. Press him in my name and kiss his fine head for me and ask him to return the kiss when I draw my dying breath. St. Joseph, patron of departed souls - pray for me. Amen.[xiii]

Journaling space for mothers:

<u>Chapter Five: Weeks 10-11</u>

<u>"Holiness consists simply in doing God's will and being just what God wants us to be." – St Therese of Lisieux[xiv]</u>

The baby grows from a size of a strawberry[xv] (10 weeks) to size of a fig (11 weeks)! The baby is getting little teeth buds at week 10 and fingers and toes are growing in more now! The baby starts to inhale and exhale the amniotic fluid around 11 weeks[xvi], which help the baby's lungs develop more! Also, at 10 weeks, the eyelids cover the eyes of the baby, and they will stay shut till around 27 weeks according to the baby center![xvii]

The mother may feel more bloating as the baby is growing and the uterus is expanding. The mother may be in kind of in between regular clothes and maternity wear. Find clothes that have elastic bands that can expand or wear a nice dress that flows!

Mother's may experience excessive saliva during this time frame – try chewing gum to swallow it easier or drink more fluids.[xviii] The "privates" area – your vagina may experience different fluid discharge that is more white or milky – this is normal.[xix] Also, more towards 11 weeks you may feel constipated and have heartburn. Both these are normal symptoms of pregnancy at this time frame.

Digestion maybe slower – try drinking fluids even in a slow way throughout the day can help![xx]

So, you are also probably still having some nausea symptoms – usually this will dissipate more closer to 12 weeks or so. However, some mothers can get a bad disease called Hyperemesis Gravidarum – where they are constantly throwing up and not able to eat very well or at all. This is highly dangerous situation, and the mother needs to seek medical help immediately if she is having this in a severe way. She may need to get food into her another way through her stomach, etc. You can read more here: https://americanpregnancy.org/healthy-pregnancy/pregnancy-complications/hyperemesis-gravidarum-880/

Doula tip: If you are a doula helping a mother earlier in her pregnancy – make sure if mom is having severe issues with throwing up that the mother seeks a doctor right away for help! The list below is some of the symptoms of *hyperemesis gravidarium:*

Severe nausea and vomiting

Food aversions

Weight loss of 5% or more of pre-pregnancy weight

Decrease in urination

Dehydration

Headaches

Confusion

Fainting

Jaundice

Extreme fatigue

Low blood pressure

Rapid heart rate

Loss of skin elasticity

Secondary anxiety/depression[xxi] (Note: We will talk about St. Dymphna as patroness of anxiety and depression in another section).

Dad Tip: If mother is experiencing any of the symptoms above – get her over to a doctor right away. Also, support her as much as possible. If she is eating something, then make sure she has that food in the house that she can tolerate!

Treatments that may help this include: (Medical):

Intravenous fluids (IV) – to restore hydration, electrolytes, vitamins, and nutrients

Tube feeding:

Nasogastric – restores nutrients through a tube passing through the nose and into the stomach. Percutaneous endoscopic gastrostomy – restores nutrients through a tube passing through the abdomen and into the stomach; requires a surgical procedure. Medications – metoclopramide, antihistamines, and anti reflux medications*[xxii]

Non-medical treatments: Bed Rest –This may provide comfort, but be cautious and aware of the effects of muscle and weight loss due to too much bed rest.

For General Nausea:

Acupressure – The pressure points to reduce nausea is located at the middle of the inner wrist, three-finger lengths away from the crease of the wrist, and between the two tendons. Locate and press firmly, one wrist at a time for three minutes. Sea bands also help with acupressure and can be found at your local drug store. Herbs – ginger or peppermint can help with nausea. However, if mother is tandem breastfeeding a toddler and pregnant then peppermint might cause her breastmilk to dry up.

Homeopathic remedies are a non-toxic system of medicines.[xxiii]

Doulas and dads are not to diagnose anything but get mom treatments as soon as possible with her health care provider. If looking for more natural treatment find a naturopathic doctor to work with if possible.

<u>Saint of Motherhood section:</u>

St. Therese and her illness as a child: St. Therese had a weird illness that no doctor could diagnosis after her sister Pauline entered Carmel. St. Therese did not lose her reason, but she did kind of have hallucinations and called out "Mama" a few times and scared her older sister Marie. St. Therese had this illness for awhile and Marie is the one who prayed to Our Lady of the Smile (the statue that also gave their mother St. Zélie Consolation at one time). As Marie was pleading for St. Therese's life, the statue looked down upon St. Therese and "smiled upon her."[xxiv] St. Therese was instantly cured of her malady! So, Our Lady of the Smile is this statue that came with St. Therese to Carmel. This Marian miracle shows us that even if things seem dark; that Our Lady can come through with simplicity of prayer. The motherly saint is Our Lady looking over her daughter St. Therese who was destined to be a great Carmelite nun! Also, I believe St. Therese was preserved from an early death, so she could teach us her "Little way" – which we will talk about more later. Part of that little way is accepting God's will at any moment during our lives!

Prayer: St. Therese, teach us how to pray better. Teach us how to lead us to our Lady. Teach us your "Little Way" to heaven, so we will fly their when we die. Amen.

<u>St. Anne Craft Section:</u>

St. Anne is also a mother we can pray to as a saint of motherhood. This is a simple craft you can make. I am sure you are reading lots of books about pregnancy. How about make a St. Anne bookmark?

1. Step one find a picture of St. Anne from the Internet you like.

2. Step two paste the picture on a page or Word document.

3. Step three make the picture the right size for a bookmark – you can decide your favorite bookmark size or go for around 2 inches wide to 8 inches long. Actually, you can make it wider if so desired. 4. Step four – print and cut it out! See below for a sample picture!

Bookmark sample – plus any other blank spaced can be used for journaling!xxv

____ (4 inches wide x 5 or so)

Journaling space continued.

Chapter 6: Weeks 12-13 of Pregnancy

"Miss no single opportunity of making some small sacrifice, here by a smiling look, there by a kindly word; always doing the smallest right and doing it all for love."-St. Therese of Lisieux.[xxvi]

A beautiful summary of her Little Way is offered in an old prayer:

"St. Therese, Little Flower, grant that I may follow your Little Way through Mary to Jesus — the way of simplicity, joy, meekness and humility of heart, devotion to my vocation, constant prayer, self-immolation, abandonment of my will to the Will of God and confidence and love in Jesus."[xxvii] *To read more about her little way go to:* https://www.bluearmy.com/the-little-way-of-st-therese-through-mary-to-jesus/

By the 12th week or so, you should be experiencing less nausea!

Baby inside of you is sucking his/her thumb now (or can do so!) The baby may also urinate now.[xxviii] (LOL!) So, maybe that's why you feel like you have to pee! Baby can curl his toes! **Baby is around size of a lime!**[xxix]

Twin pregnancy! We thought we would talk a little bit about twins for this section. Twins are fun! However, if you are a twin pregnancy – you will probably be experiencing more heartburn esp. at 12 weeks.[xxx] This is due to the growing

placenta and uterus – so need more room for 2 babies inside of you!!

<u>**Week 13 Pregnancy:**</u>[xxxi]

The baby's fingerprints are forming – no two fingerprints are alike! The baby is around size of a peapod (as far as length goes). Or another site says your baby is size of a large plum![xxxii]

"Your baby's intestines have moved back into the abdomen from the

umbilical cord, now that there's enough room to accommodate them, and some of

the larger bones, including those of the skull, are beginning to harden.

What else is happening with your baby? Even though you won't hear those

tiny coos and cries until after you give birth, your baby's little vocal cords have

already started to develop."[xxxiii]

<u>Twins!</u> Here is some information about types of twins:

"Fraternal twins. This is when two eggs are fertilized by two different sperm, creating two zygotes, each of which becomes an embryo. Fraternal twins will not be identical and can be either the same sex or a boy and a girl.

Identical twins. This is when only one egg is fertilized, and the zygote splits into two early in pregnancy, forming two embryos. Identical twins have the same chromosomes and will look the same and be the same sex."[xxxiv]

If you are a *mother preparing to have twins*, then you may want to know more about breastfeeding twins and how to care for them. Most mothers can breastfeed twins just fine; however, supplementation maybe recommended just in case. Always consult a lactation specialist or consultant to find out more information on what is recommended. Pumping your milk maybe a good idea if you are expecting twins – that way after breastfeeding is established well (around a month) then you can also pump and give a bottle occasionally if needed. Pumping can start immediately after birth but introducing a bottle should wait unless one baby is not getting enough milk! Also, if the twins are born premature then of course follow the doctor's suggestions on pumping and giving bottles, etc.

The best position for breastfeeding twins is the "football" hold position _ please see picture.[xxxv]

This position you hold the infant much like a football. You may want a nursing pillow or two to help hold up the baby at breast level. It is best to make sure baby is not twisted when nursing. Always have the baby line up with his/her tummy next to your body! Other positions maybe the crisscross hold and football together can also be used. If you are not familiar with baby breastfeeding positions here is some pictures of all breastfeeding positions below!

So, the most common positions are cradle position, cross-cradle, football hold, laid-back position, and side-lying position for breastfeeding. Do you need a breastfeeding specialist? Go to www.mommylatch.com to learn about breastfeeding counselor-educators. Also the IBLC website should have a list of lactation consultants.

Dad Boot Camp Tip for Twins: Dad's should be included in planning of any birth. Will he help cut the cord? Will he be able to get off work for close to the due date? Will this be a planned C-section? Make sure you write down your birthing plan ideas for dad to participate! Write down one way dad will participate in the birth (either singleton or twin):

Doula Tip Section: If you are supporting Twins for birth, then prepare mother for various circumstances – make sure you do research on twin births. However, mothers can have a natural birth for twin pregnancy. If she wants a natural birth, we strongly recommend finding a midwife that can help with this. Usually if the twin A is not breech baby, a midwife is more willing to help with the pregnancy of twins. However, one can attempt to move a breech baby as well – researching that at www.spinningbabies.com.

<u>Motherhood saint and St. Anne Craft:</u>

St. Emilia, Amelia, or Emily: She was a mother of 10 children! I thought this would be a great saint for mothers to look too! Five of her children are canonized saints. In fact both the Catholic Church and Orthodox claim St. Emilia as their saint! Here's a little more of her story:

"Most notably, St. Emilia was the mother to Saint Basil the Great. She was also mother to St. Macrina, St. Peter of Sebaste, St. Gregory of Nyssa, and St. Theosebia. When she had her children, her first and only job was to instill the Holy Orthodox faith in them. She taught them how to pray to God. She also taught and showed them how they could live their life in service of Him.

In her life, she suffered one of the greatest heartaches as a mother; she lost one of her children. This was devastating to her, but her youngest daughter St. Macrina came to her aide by reminding her to take comfort in the Lord. When all of her children were grown, St. Emilia decided to leave her home to find a monastery in a secluded area. Her youngest daughter Macrina came with her."[xxxvi] So, St. Emilia became a type of hermit – but this ended up growing to a group of other nuns and she basically founded a monastery!

So, what can we learn from this saint as far as motherhood goes? She kept faithful to helping her children grow up in the Christian (Catholic) faith! She made sure they were taken care of before leaving and starting a hermitage! Emilia reminds me of a type of Carmelite spirituality like our St. Therese. Carmelites are mini hermits. They spend a lot of their day in prayer in their cells or in the chapel in adoration! Though there were duties for each Carmelite sister – they all kept to a strict prayer life. I remember reading that when a bell rings in a convent – the nuns are to stop what they are doing like at recreation – even in mid-sentence and put away their things (like if they were sewing) and go immediately to prayer or whatever task was next on their list of things to do that day. Isn't that amazing?! If we would even practice this a bit of reflection and recollection during the day – we may benefit from a closer connection to Jesus and Mary! Write down a thought from this plus extra journaling space:

St. Anne's Craft Corner! Make an icon!

How to draw or paint an icon saint: https://www.wikihow.com/Draw-Orthodox-Icons Tutorial on how to draw:

https://www.youtube.com/watch?v=S_RSk2eDpmo

Here is another link on drawing:

https://www.monasteryicons.com/product/How-an-Icon-is-Painted/did-you-know

Here is another show you how to paint an icon: https://www.atelier-st-andre.net/en/pages/technique/icon_technique/icon_painting.html

We suggest making a simple icon for your baby! If you have a baby name – maybe look up the saint and draw the saint in an icon for the baby or use Jesus or Mary as a simpler idea to use.

Journaling space:

<u>Chapter Seven: Week 14-15 of Pregnancy!</u>

<u>"I can nourish myself on nothing but truth."</u>

<u>-St. Therese of Lisieux.</u>[xxxvii]

I thought we could focus more on nutrition for mothers for this section of our book! First, we will talk about baby growth, etc.

As your baby is growing into a rubber ducky size[xxxviii] – you are now officially in the 2nd trimester of pregnancy – congratulations! The baby is moving around more, and you might even feel the first movements of your child anytime now – or up to 16 weeks. I think I remember one of my pregnancies I felt movement around this time frame of around 14-15 weeks.

Private talk: If you feel like your "sex drive" is back[xxxix] – that is great, and a married mother may want to get together with her husband more now – sex during pregnancy will not hurt the baby as long as your waters have not broken (like in the last trimester) and your doctor doesn't say "no." Nourishing your sex life is just as important as food too!

So, talking about food and pregnancy – your appetite should be better now that you have reached the second trimester and you are probably wondering –

"can I eat this or that?" Are eggs ok to eat? Yes, eggs are an excellent source of choline which is necessary for baby development and part of the B vitamin family.

If you want to really learn more about nutrition and pregnancy, we recommend Lily Nichols' book "The Real Food for Pregnancy" and you can get the first chapter free by going to this link:

https://realfoodforpregnancy.com/bonus/

We also know of a mini course that is for doulas or mamas as well that teaches you about nutrition for pregnancy and doulas who take it get a certified Nutritional doula status. http://nutritionaldoula.com for more information. There's also various other nutrition classes – so just do a general search if interested in this topic.

Recipes from Lily's website: https://lilynicholsrdn.com/real-food-postpartum-recovery-meals/ Most of the recipes are for postpartum; however, you can probably eat most of that during pregnancy as well. We suggest trying out a few recipes now and then making and freezing the food recipes you like the best during your third trimester!! Freezing foods for postpartum recovery is the best idea to help you be able to relax and not worry about "one thing" postpartum! Another thing is you can hire someone to come in and cook all the food for you if so desired! Also, if you just want to do it yourself – maybe hire a nutritional doula to take a look at your pantry and help you with meal planning! That is one thing a nutritional doula does! A nutritional doula can help during pregnancy esp. if a mother is on bedrest. So, if you are a mother on bedrest you may want to consider hiring a doula to come in for the cooking aspect of things now! Also, some postpartum doulas may also offer this service of making meals (but most likely only for postpartum time frame).

Here are a few tips for nutrition for mothers:

Eat high protein meals – chicken, fish, beef (organic if possible), beans.

Eat rice with beans for full protein.

Whole grains over non-whole grains.

Eat less carbs esp. if diabetic or pre-diabetic.

Eat vegetables! Choose a great variety!

If doing dairy products, keep organic as possible!

Ok, hope this list helps with meal planning!

St. Anne Cooking Section:

Our special feature this time is St. Anne and cooking! We want you to have fun with any recipes or crafts.

Mother Bowl Recipe:[xl]

Cook up Basmati or Brown rice set aside. Cook a chicken in a crockpot or Instant Pot. Cook vegetables – fry, grill or boil (depending on how chewy you like your veggies). Mix together the chicken, rice and vegetables in a bowl! Serve with your favorite green tea or raspberry leaf tea!

Variety: Change up the meat, change up veggies each day, choose another grain like millet, grits, quinoa, potatoes (occasionally), noodles, etc.

Doula Tip and Nutrition:

Doulas should check in with mother to see how she is eating. Have mom do a food diary. Remember you are not diagnosing anything – however, a friendly suggestion on foods can help a mother change her diet. Also, suggest she talk to her doctor if she's having issues digesting foods. She may need some gut repair – but being pregnant – she may need to see what she can eat or take for that or not. Mothers may like the encouragement from a doula; others may not – be sensitive to the mother's needs.

Dad Boot Camp Tip and Nutrition: Make sure mom is drinking enough fluids and eating properly – help cook a meal once a week to help out! You should also consider closer to third trimester to organize a meal planning group with your community. If your Catholic Church has something, then organize a meal train through them. Most churches will have an organized way to give mom's meals after having a baby! They will usually organize freezer meals and then distribute them on certain dates or have the mother's family pick up at the parish. If your parish does not have this yet, this might be something that the "guys" can suggest to their wives to help organize. New dads also need support – so think of one way you may want that support – perhaps a "date night" with your wife and arrange babysitting for instance!

Think of one way you can get time with your wife after birth and how you will accomplish this:

<u>Saint of Motherhood and Eating!</u>

<u>If a mother has an eating disorder she should pray to St. Catherine of Siena.</u>
St. Catherine of Siena was a mystic that lived a while back and she was a Dominican Third Order member. So, she lived at home with her family. She at one time fasted for a very long time and lived solely on The Holy Eucharist. During these times she could not tolerate even eating some herbs and such according to some accounts.[xli] She fasted this way to make up for the sins of gluttony![xlii] Other accounts say St. Catherine did eat herbs and water and then she died at age 33. Also, St. Rose of Lima fasted quite a bit and also died at a young age as well.[xliii] So, is it possible that these saints also had an eating disorder? Well, possibly but God allowed them to fast and/or be sick for a reason to make up for sins of others! If a mother is throwing up her food and not getting enough to eat – one should be alarmed esp. after the first trimester – mother may have an eating disorder and need to see a doctor and get IV's or other medical treatments. <u>Doula tip:</u> If you notice a mother is not eating properly, tell the husband or partner so this mother can get help she needs!

If you are a mother and suspect that you may have an eating disorder, pray to St. Catherine of Siena and/or St. Rose of Lima if you have an eating disorder and contact your doctor to get help! Prayer: St. Catherine of Siena, please help me to eat properly and give God the designs of my will to do His will in eating a proper diet. Amen. Read more about here: https://en.wikipedia.org/wiki/Anorexia_mirabilis and https://en.wikipedia.org/wiki/Anorexia_nervosa

St. Rose of Lima, beautiful Lily of God, give me hope to overcome any food eating difficulties and be able to bless God with all my heart. Amen.

<u>St. Joseph Smoothie Recipes:</u>

Banana Smoothie:

1 cup cold milk

2 ripe bananas

1 cup cracked ice or 1 cup vanilla ice cream

Blend to desired consistency.

St. Anne Berry Smoothie:

1/2 cup diluted apple juice (diluted in half)

1-1/2 cups fresh strawberries, washed

2-1/2 to 3 cups ice

Sugar to taste

Blend together apple juice, strawberries, and sugar until smooth. Strain.

Add ice and blend again until smooth and thick.

Room for Journaling about the second trimester start (picture credit)[xliv]:

Chapter Eight: Pregnancy: Week 16-17

"By becoming little and weak for me, [Jesus] made me strong and full of courage, and with the arms He gave me, I went from one victory to another, and began to 'run as a giant'" (Ps.18:16). St. Therese[xlv]

Your little baby is like St. Therese – a "little, small one" inside of you right now. However, your heart as a mother can "run as a giant" into the arms of Jesus and Mary and ask them for help!

Avocado size is your baby at week 16. "Your fetus is becoming a looker too — with a face that's starting to look more human — but a skinny looker, since there's no baby fat yet. Listen up: tiny bones in your fetus' ears are in place, making it likely that baby can hear your voice (or something like it) when you're speaking at 16 weeks pregnant. In fact, studies have found that babies who hear a song while they're in the womb recognize the same tune when it's sung to them after they're born — so choose your lullabies with that in mind."[xlvi]

Week 17 baby is a size of a turnip or potato! Around this stage of pregnancy, the fetus starts to look a lot more human. "In addition to hair growing on the head, the eyebrows and eyelashes are also developing. The eyelids are shut, but the eyes themselves can move and the mouth can also open and close. The fingernails and toenails are growing, and your bundle of joy has also developed a firm grip! Your baby's been getting bigger and bigger over the last couple of weeks, and this means that he or she has needed a larger placenta. Remember that the placenta is the organ that supplies nutrition to the fetus, removes waste products, and fulfills other important roles. By the end of your pregnancy, the placenta will weigh around 18 oz (510 g)."[xlvii]

Your body at week 16-17: Mama – your body will look more pregnant, and you may be showing more! If you are experiencing nasal congestion – just another thing to attribute to pregnancy. You may want to try diffusing some essential oil blends (see crafting section below!) There's an upside too: "at this stage of pregnancy, many women start to take on a glow that results from an increase in blood volume and a surge of hormones. This can mean glossy, thick hair and radiant skin. You may not feel very glamorous, but don't be surprised if your partner notices!"[xlviii]

Journal some now below about weeks 16-17 and how your little one is growing – do you feel movement yet?

Journaling space below:

St. Anne Crafting Corner plus doula tip section

Make an essential oil blend for relaxation and diffuse it!

<u>Doula Tip:</u> If you are a doula helping a mom prenatally – and mom wants to use essential oils – always have her test her skin to see if she has any allergic reactions before using on her body or dilute and see if that helps any. If she has major reaction, do not use that oil on her! Pure essential oils are also important – we recommend 3 companies that offer great pure oils: Young Living Essential Oils, Simply Earth Essential Oils, and Ancient Wisdom Essential Oils. Simply Earth has a subscription box, and it is a non-MLM style place – so if you don't like multi-level marketing, we recommend that company!

www.simplyearth.com

Suggestions on how to dilute oils – usually it is a 1% to 5% ratio of "carrier oil" to essential oils. We suggest you read this article:

https://livewellzone.com/how-to-dilute-essential-oils/ for dilution instructions!

We are not listing specific combinations of oils as there are a lot of oils that cannot be used during pregnancy. There are some safe essential oils as well that a mother can use. You may want to read this article:

https://www.healthline.com/health/pregnancy/essential-oils-for-pregnancy

Avoid list of essential oils – do not use these[xlix]:

Fennel, Clary sage, Sage, Marjoram

Tarragon, Caraway, Cinnamon

Thuja, Mugwort, Birch, Wintergreen

Basil (estragole CT), Camphor

Hyssop, Aniseed, Tansy

Wormwood, Parsley seed or leaf, Pennyroyal

<u>Dad Tip:</u> Best way for pregnant mother to use essential oils is through the air! Buy a diffuser and she can smell her favorite scents throughout the day like lavender, lemon, eucalyptus, etc. This lessens the opportunity for any reactions by diffusing essential oils! Mother can also put oils on a cotton ball in her room as well as get a small diffuser if driving around in her car. Doulas should also remember above tip – esp. during labor – diffusing is the best and safest way!

Saint of Motherhood

Saint Agatha – patroness of breast ailments![1]

Saint Agatha has been venerated as a virgin and martyr since the time of her death in AD 251. Besides the Blessed Virgin Mary, she is only one of seven women saints commemorated in the Roman Canon (Eucharistic Prayer 1) and as early as the fifth century had two churches in Rome dedicated to her. Born in Sicily to a noble family, Agatha was a devout Christian who dedicated her virginity to God. Pursued by Quintianus, a prefect or governor, she rebuffed his advances. He had Agatha arrested for being a Christian and forced her to renounce Christ.

Her documented writings of her speaks of the brutal interrogations and torture she endured at his hand. When she refused, she was imprisoned in a brothel, then a prison, stretched on the rack, burned with red hot irons and had her breasts cut off. She had an apparition of St. Peter as a physician and was miraculously healed of her wounds. Four days later upon further interrogation and to the surprise of her torturers, she was condemned to death by rolling her naked body in broken glass and hot coals. At the very moment of her final torture a great earthquake struck the region. Immediately before her death Saint Agatha was heard praying, "O Lord Jesus Christ, good Master, I give You thanks that You granted me victory over the executioners' tortures. Grant now that I may happily dwell in Your never-ending glory".[li]

Saint Agatha[lii] is the patron saint of breast cancer. *Prayer to Saint Agatha*:

O Heavenly Father, Who raised Agatha to the dignity of Sainthood, we implore Your Divine Majesty by her intercession to give us health of mind, body and soul.

Free us from all those things which hold us bound to this earth, and let our spirit, like hers, rise to your heavenly courts. Through Jesus Christ, Your Son, our Lord, Who lives and reigns with You, forever. Amen.

Journaling space below:

<u>Chapter 9: Weeks 18-19</u>

<u>Weeks 18-19 of Pregnancy "Jesus, help me to simplify my life by learning what you want me to be and becoming that person." – St Therese of Lisieux[liii]</u>

<u>St. Therese</u>'s little way – we want to talk about it a little more now before going into the next weeks of pregnancy.

St. Therese wants to lead us to God in her "Little Way" to heaven. This little way is simply doing the will of God in our everyday things – from being a pregnant mother to changing the baby's first diapers! Doing things with love – giving God our love in our daily tasks. And yes, doing it without complaint. Ah, I know this later is harder to do – sometimes we still complain – but we should stop and give

God our Love! So, let's go to Jesus to ask Him to help us be the best mother possible to our little one inside the womb!

Meditation: Imagine Baby Jesus inside of Mary's womb. He's there for 9 months growing inside of Our Lady. Mary travels to visit Elizabeth as part of her desires to help her cousin during her pregnancy as well. When Jesus meets St. John the Baptist in his mother's womb – St. John Leaps for Joy! Elizabeth relates this to Mary that her "baby lept in her womb for joy" – and Mary's response is the wonderful "Magnificat" prayer! Meditate on this visit for a few minutes each day of your journey as a pregnant mother.

Week 18-19 – almost halfway through your pregnancy! This maybe the week(s) that you go into get an ultrasound for the first time (if you have not done so yet). I believe this was when we got our first ultrasound of our daughter. Since they had a discrepancy of her due date after viewing the ultrasound – we went back one month later. Both said she was due a little later – so we figured that I probably got pregnant a little later then what we had thought! My original due date of August 5th was moved to August 23rd! I also measured closer to the newer due date – so we knew we were on track for the right timing!

<u>Doula tip</u>: If you are going in to get an ultrasound, and if you have a doula, bring your doula with you! She may like the opportunity to support you during an ultrasound – also good if there is bad news (but hopefully not!)

<u>Doulas if you accompany a mother with an ultrasound</u> – do not overstep your authority – remember you are not a doctor and not allowed to discuss medical things – if there is something wrong help the mother get the doctor to get answers right away. Perhaps, the tech saw that the baby will have Down Syndrome for instance. This is a diagnosis that some mothers maybe shocked to hear; so make sure you are there for that mother and help her with any emotional side of things (this is just for instance scenario).

Mama, you will be seeing your baby "inside for the first time" – have fun counting the toes if you can see them or at least see the little hand waving at you! Make sure you get the little pictures printed out of your ultrasound! Remember to make a keepsake print off to put in your journal here below!! (There will be room on the journaling page to post a picture). Mama if you have any questions for your doctor during this time, make sure you have them written down before you arrive. All I remember is having to drink a whole bunch of water and be uncomfortable while they did the ultrasound because they didn't want me to pee till afterwards.

(LOL!) Ugh!! I think I ended up having to go first and then drink a little more water before they saw me! So, be prepared for lots of water that day if you are doing this!

Dad tip and mama tip together: You both need to decide on this – are you going to find out the gender at this ultrasound or not? It is not good for one of you to be in disagreement -so decide together and stick with the decision!!

Journaling section about this time frame:

<u>St. Anne Crafting section:</u>

Take the ultrasound picture you get and decorate it in a special way and put it in a family album! Check off if you did this: ________.

If you are choosing not to go get an ultrasound right now, then think of a family photo session during this pregnant time – take a picture of your growing belly and post it in your family album: _________. (Or do both!!)

Journaling space:

<u>Motherhood Saint: Our Lady of Guadalupe – patroness of the unborn</u>

<u>Brief history of Our Lady of Guadalupe</u>[liv]**<u>;</u>**

<u>Original words from the apparitions:</u>

First apparition; December 9 – Quote below[lv]:

Juanito, dearest Juan Diego. Juanito, my dearest son, where are you going? Know and understand well, you my most humble son, that I am the ever-virgin Holy Mary, Mother of the True God for whom we live, of the Creator of all things, Lord of heaven and the earth. I wish that a temple be erected here quickly, so I may therein exhibit and give all my love, compassion, help, and protection, because I am your merciful mother, to you, and to all the inhabitants on this land and all the rest who love me, invoke and confide in me; listen there to their lamentations, and remedy all their miseries, afflictions and sorrows. And to accomplish what my clemency pretends, go to the palace of the bishop of Mexico, and you will say to him that I manifest my great desire, that here on this plain a temple be built to me; you will accurately relate all you have seen and admired, and what you have heard. Be assured that I will be most grateful and will reward you, because I will make you happy and worthy of recompense for the effort and fatigue in what you will obtain of what I have entrusted. Behold, you have heard my mandate, my humble son; go and put forth all your effort."

Second apparition; December 9

Hark, my little son, you must understand that I have many servants and messengers, to whom I must entrust the delivery of my message, and carry my wish, but it is of precise detail that you yourself solicit and assist and that through your mediation my wish be complied. I earnestly implore, my son the least, and with sternness I command that you again go tomorrow and see the bishop. You go in my name and make known my wish in its entirety that he has to start the erection of a temple which I ask of him. And again tell him that I, in person, the ever-virgin Holy Mary, Mother of God, sent you." (Temple means church in our language).

Fourth apparition; December 12

"Hear me and understand well, my little son, that nothing should frighten or grieve you. Let not your heart be disturbed. Do not fear that sickness, nor any other sickness or anguish. Am I not here, who is your Mother? Are you not under my protection? Am I not your health? Are you not happily within my fold? What else do you wish? Do not grieve nor be disturbed by anything. Do not be afflicted by the illness of your uncle, who will not die now of it. Be assured that he is now cured. Climb, my dear son, to the top of the hill; there where you saw me and I gave you orders, you will find different flowers. Cut them, gather them, assemble them, then come and bring them before my presence. My dear little son, this diversity of roses is the proof and the sign which you will take to the bishop. You will tell him in my name that he will see in them my wish and that he will have to comply to it. You are my ambassador, most worthy of all confidence. Rigorously I command you that only before the presence of the bishop will you unfold your mantle and disclose what you are carrying. You will relate all and well; you will tell that I ordered you to climb to the hilltop, to go and cut flowers; and all that you saw and admired, so you can induce the prelate to give his support, with the aim that a temple be built and erected as I have asked."

To read further about the historical context of the miracle of Our Lady of Guadalupe, we suggest the contemporaneous account of Bernal Diaz, The Conquest of New Spain. Our Lady as the woman "who will crush the head of the serpent" is also the destroyer of all heresies and error and consoled by this truth of her motherly protection, we confidently approach her with the words: Our Lady of Guadalupe, pray for us![lvi]

Our short summary is below:

On December 12, 1531, the Blessed Virgin Mary spoke to a humble native in his own Nahuatl tongue. The exact sound that met the Mexican's ears was "Juanito, Juan Diegito." It was an endearing expression that a fond mother would use for her child. English would render it: "Dear little Juan."

She motioned Juan to come closer. Advancing a step or two he sank to his knees, overwhelmed by the loveliness of the vision. The beautiful lady requested that a shrine be built and dedicated to her on the Hill of Tepeyac. Speaking to him in the native language, Our Lady called herself "of Guadalupe," a Spanish name meaning the one "who crushes the serpent."

Sadly, the bishop refused to believe that the Mother of God would appear to a poor, illiterate Mexican like Juan. Juan returned to the place of the apparition where Our Lady again appeared. She told him to return the next morning when she would give him a sign that would convince the bishop of the truth of her appearance and her request.[lvii]

The following morning Our Lady told Juan to go to the top of the hill and gather Castilian roses that he would find there. Although he knew that only cactus grew there, he obeyed, and his simple faith was rewarded by the sight of beautiful roses growing where she had told him they would be.

He gathered them and showed them to Our Lady who rearranged them for him, placing them in his cloak or "tilma." Juan returned to the bishop. As he opened his tilma, the roses fell to the floor. All who were present were startled to see an image of Our Lady of Guadalupe clearly imprinted on the tilma.

Today this image is still preserved on Juan Diego's tilma, which hangs over the main altar in the basilica at the foot of Tepeyac Hill just outside of Mexico City.[lviii]

In the image, Our Lady is pregnant, carrying the Son of God in her womb. Her head is bowed in homage, indicating that she is not a goddess, but rather the one who bears and at the same time worships the one true God.

The Serpent's Head Is Crushed

When Mary first appeared to Blessed Juan Diego, Mexico had been in the hands of Christian leaders for only a short time. Human sacrifice, where the blood of innocents was often spilled to appease the thirsty demons of the old rite, was still practiced. The Aztec priests executed annually at least 50,000 inhabitants of the land — men, women, and children — in human sacrifices to their gods. In 1487, just in a single four-day ceremony for the dedication of a new temple in Tenochtitlan, some 80,000 captives were killed in human sacrifice. The same practices, which in most cases included the cannibalism of the victims' limbs, were common also in earlier Mesoamerican cultures, with widespread Olmec, Toltec and Mayan human sacrificing rituals.

Children were said to be frequent victims, in part because they were considered pure and unspoiled. The early Mexican historian Ixtlilxochitl estimated that one out of every five children in Mexico were sacrificed. Into this cavern of darkness and ignorance, our Lady of Guadalupe brought a message of maternal compassion:

"I am the merciful Mother, the mother of all of you who live united in this land, and of all mankind, of all those who love me, of those who cry to me, of those who seek me, of those who have confidence in me. Here I will hear their weeping, their sorrow, and will remedy and alleviate their suffering, necessities, and misfortunes."

By 1541, just ten years after the apparitions, there were ten million Indians who had been converted from paganism. Before Our Lady's coming the missionaries were able to pour the saving waters of Baptism upon the heads of only one million natives, and most of these were orphaned children, victims of war, whom the loving missionaries had adopted and educated. Such a mass conversion was an unprecedented phenomenon, the likes of which had never been witnessed in any country of the world.

How much our nation still needs her message of compassion! Let us together pray for the assistance and protection of Our Lady of Guadalupe. Her face radiates the very light of God, while her example reveals authentic femininity. She shows unparalleled compassion to the poor and defenseless, but unyielding power and triumph over the evil one and his cohorts.[lix]

<u>Prayer to Our Lady of Guadalupe:</u>

Remember, O most gracious Virgin Mary of Guadalupe, that in thy celestial apparitions on the mount of Tepeyac, thou didst promise to show thy compassion and pity towards all who, loving and trusting thee, seek thy help and call upon thee in their necessities and afflictions.

Thou didst promise to hearken to our supplications, to dry our tears and to give us consolation and relief. Never was it known that anyone who fled to thy protection, implored thy help, or sought thy intercession, either for the common welfare, or in personal anxieties, was left unaided.

Inspired with this confidence, we fly unto thee, O Mary, ever Virgin Mother of the True God! Though grieving under the weight of our sins, we come to prostrate ourselves in thy august presence, certain that thou wilt deign to fulfill thy merciful promises. We are full of hope that, standing beneath thy shadow and protection, nothing will trouble or afflict us, nor need we fear illness, or misfortune, or any other sorrow.

Thou hast decided to remain with us through thy admirable image, thou who art our mother, our health and our life. Placing ourselves beneath thy maternal gaze and having recourse to thee in all our necessities we need do nothing more. O Holy Mother of God, despise not our petitions, but in thy mercy hear and answer us. (Here mention your petition.) Amen.

Five Hail Mary's...in gratitude for the four apparitions to Juan Diego and the one to Juan Bernardino.[lx]

<u>Chapter 10: Pregnancy Week 20-21</u>

<u>"I have not the courage to force myself to seek beautiful prayers in books; not knowing which to choose I act as children do who cannot read; I say quite simply to the good God what I want to tell Him, and He always understands me."</u>

<u>St. Therese</u>[lxi]

St. Therese's simplicity and purity of heart are evident in this quote. So many of us complicate our lives. We see this in the media as people constantly analyze and overcompensate. Science is secular society's religion, and the world of academia has become our god. But St. Therese[lxii] says we don't need fancy words or even beautiful, complex analyses of theories in order to reach God. In fact, it's quite the contrary. What we need is the heart of a child – ever-available to God's presence, speaking plainly and from the heart. It's the heart language that speaks to God above all other complex conversation.[lxiii]

Wow, congratulations – you are now halfway through your pregnancy now! Your little "baby bean" is growing more! Dad can probably feel the baby kicking or soon in your belly. Have him put his hand on your belly and feel! You probably look more "pregnant" now and may need some maternity clothes now. Are you looking for modest maternity clothes? Look in the St. Anne section for some resources.

Week 20 – your baby is the size of a bell pepper!

Week 21 – your baby is the size of a banana (I guess they are slightly longer than a bell pepper!)

At week 20 – the baby's digestive system is working better now and well hey, that first "baby poop" called meconium is starting to develop now (yuck!) Usually, the baby will pass this during the first diaper change or two – however, some babies poop during delivery – that is usually called "meconium staining". This can happen if infant is under "stress" during delivery. Most of the time the baby is fine – it may just take a little extra care and cleanup after the birth! However, meconium aspiration can occur, and the baby may have to go to NICU. If you want to read more about this condition go:

https://www.verywellfamily.com/meconium-babys-first-stool-2759060 Please do not worry about this – and pray to St. Anthony and St. Gerard Majella for a good delivery!

Week 21 development: Around 21 weeks the baby's fingers and toes are completely developed and will have unique fingerprints and toe prints! (Most mothers look forward to seeing the newborn baby footprints that are taken by the hospital!) The baby is now able to swallow the amniotic fluid since his/her digestive system is more up and running! The baby can produce his/her own blood cells now as well!

Mom may feel baby move for the first time at 20 weeks – this is also called "quickening."[lxiv] Some more fun facts from the pampers site: "If you have a checkup at 20 weeks, your healthcare provider may measure the distance from your pubic bone to the top of the uterus, which is called the fundus. This fundal height measurement gives your provider information about your baby's growth. At around 20 weeks of pregnancy, the top of the uterus reaches the navel, and your fundal height would be about 7 to 8.5 inches (18 to 22 centimeters). Here's a fun fact about the fundal height measurement: Your fundal height in centimeters is roughly equal to the number of weeks you are pregnant!"[lxv]

Week 21: Your pregnancy hormones maybe kicking in more – you may experience more of the following symptoms as a pregnant mother[lxvi]:

*Backache

*Heartburn

*Hot flashes

*Stretch marks

*Leg cramps

The website (pampers) suggests[lxvii] that the mother take B vitamins for support on energy – we add in – please ask your doctor or midwife before taking supplements! However, B vitamins should help with some energy levels!

Another recommendation: Find a good chiropractor if you are having back issues and get adjusted regularly during pregnancy. There are some chiropractors who specialize in Webster Technique which is something more specific for pregnancy. Chiropractors come in all shapes and sizes – so ask around about Webster or another technique called Zone Technique. The Zone Technique helps clear out blockages of a particular health system for instance nervous system, etc. There are not that many Zone Technique chiropractors, but they are great for balancing your body!

Choline is another nutrient that is important for pregnancy, and you can find that in eggs – so a mother should be eating eggs as part of her daily diet. If you want to read more about nutrition: we highly suggest "The Real Food for

Pregnancy" book by Lily Nichols or "Real Food for Diabetes" by same author. See the St. Anne section for a fun recipe!

Journal some pregnancy things below:

<u>Saint Anne's Corner!</u>

In our corner this time – we first have a recipe that calls for eggs! Get that choline in your diet!

Enough for one person:

2-3 eggs

Onions chopped

Garlic powder ½ tsp.

Salt to taste (or ½ tsp.) plus oil of your choice for cooking!

Place oil in a frying pan (warm oil up).

Add your onions. Fry onions till translucent (try not to burn).

Add in eggs and garlic powder and salt. Stir frequently – make like a scrambled eggs unless you like omelet style. Take off hot burner when done to your liking! Serve with toast. Enjoy!!

Another thing we mentioned above was finding maternity clothes at reasonable pricing and modest ones. Well, first of all some dresses that are not labeled maternity can work – like empire dresses or maxi dresses can be used for maternity wear. You may want to look at www.poshmark.com or www.ebay.com for some clothes!

Making modest clothing is another idea – you can probably adapt most patterns to fit a little longer or looser (depending on the style of pattern). If you know how to sew – then taking advantage of that skill can help save you on clothes. However, fabrics are not "cheap" these days – so subscribe to fabric.com, joann.com, Nick of Time Fabrics, etc. to be alerted to the best deals of the week. I never buy anything unless it is on sale!! So, that goes for fabric too! If you want some fun patterns that are based on older fashions go to Sensibility Patterns – here's an example of one dress that might be adaptable to pregnancy:

https://www.sensibility.com/shop/1909-edwardian-dress-epattern

If you are wanting to get a better idea or fuller list of modest dresses and patterns, you may want to check out this blog at

http://littlewayofmary.weebly.com

St. Jacinto Marto: Saint of Modesty and good patroness for mothers seeking modesty:

Here's a little unknown fact – that Our Lady appeared to Jacinta Marto after the main Fatima apparitions. She wanted certain messages to be known through Jacinta. One of these messages is about modesty.

Quote: *Heaven too, warned us to offer a "firm and courageous resistance to the styles and customs," for Our Lady of Fatima told blessed Jacinta Marto in 1919:*

"Certain fashions are to be introduced which will offend Our Lord very much. Those who serve God should not follow these fashions. The Church has no fashions. Our Lord is always the same."[lxviii]

Here are some other saint quotes on modesty[lxix]*:*

"You carry your snare everywhere and spread your nets in all places. You allege that you never invited others to sin. You did not indeed, by your words, but you have done so by your dress and your deportment." — Saint John Chrysostom

"Either we must speak as we dress, or dress as we speak. Why do we profess one thing and display another? The tongue talks of chastity, but the whole body reveals impurity." — Saint Jerome

"Let your modesty be a sufficient incitement, yea, an exhortation to everyone to be at peace on their merely looking at you." — Saint Ignatius of Loyola

"A pure soul is like a fine pearl. As long as it is hidden in the shell, at the bottom of the sea, no one thinks of admiring it. But if you bring it into the sunshine, this pearl will shine and attract all eyes. Thus the pure soul, which is hidden from the eyes of the world, will one day shine before the Angels in the sunshine of eternity."

— Saint John Vianney

Let us pray to these saints of modesty to help us keep ourselves in check and not follow the "fashions" of the world. "St. Jacinto Marto, please preserve us in purity of mind, body, and soul and help us choose the wardrobe that Mary would approve of when we go out in public. Amen."[lxx]

Blank for notes:

<u>**Chapter Eleven: End of 2nd Trimester Weeks 22-27:**</u>

St. Therese's quote about the Eucharist: *"Do you realize that Jesus is there in the tabernacle expressly for you – for you alone? He burns with the desire to come into your heart… Don't listen to the demon; laugh at him, and go without fear to receive the Jesus of peace and love."*[lxxi]

We have decided to write the remainder of this book in trimester sections. It is just simpler to finish the book this way! And we will also analyze our quote from St. Therese in the saint section a bit more!

<u>The second trimester</u>, you are usually feeling like going out more and doing things. If you have felt like throwing up all the time in first trimester, you are probably relieved to be able to do more things now. This is a good time to go out to eat more with your husband. Try out a new restaurant each week if you can. I remember my first pregnancy; we would go out to eat about once a week. We kind of had our favorite restaurant – Red Lobster. However, the last time we went there, we both got very ill. We think it was either food related or possibly the server went to work sick – either way, we swore never to go back to Red Lobster again. Funny thing is I probably have been a couple of times since then, but only ate soup! I

always loved their cheese biscuits! Anyway, couples should take time for "self-care" a bit more during pregnancy.

The baby keeps growing inside you during your second trimester, so some cultures have weird things or ideas about pregnancy. Some are just "old wives tales" and are not true – like don't raise your hands over your head "the baby's cord will wrap around the neck" is just nonsense! However, exploring cultural "tales" or traditions can make part of your pregnancy "waiting time" a fun thing to consider.

Cultural links: https://www.pregnancybirthbaby.org.au/cultural-practices-and-preferences-when-having-a-baby

https://www.thebump.com/a/birth-traditions-around-the-world

https://www.whattoexpect.com/pregnancy/pregnancy-birth-traditions-around-world

American Indians: https://www.babygaga.com/15-pregnancy-and-birthing-traditions-in-the-aboriginal-culture/

Philippines: https://bastyr.edu/news/general-news/2017/08/birth-culture-philippines

<u>Cultural project idea:</u> If you are curious to learn more about your culture or your husband's culture – you can look up articles about either one from the Internet. You can choose to learn the full history or just choose areas like pregnancy, babies, and parenting. A lot of cultures have "naming ceremonies." Think of one thing you would like to do as a couple that would be part of your heritage or culture for your baby. It also might be something you do when the child is older. For instance Mexican culture has a special party when a little girl turns 15, she has a quinceañera party. It is her time to shine and it is considered her "coming of age" party. Write down what you would like to do for your child either as a baby or older below:

<u>**Saint Section: St. Therese and The Eucharist.**</u>

Jesus is also our special friend and part of the Blessed Trinity in Heaven. We should go to Him more often to the Tabernacle and pray. Even if we cannot attend Mass, there are plenty of empty churches where God lives in the Eucharist, and we should go and pray at one weekly or daily if possible. Remember to pray for a friend or relative in need. Pray for the Holy Souls in purgatory. Pray for mothers and those called to motherhood! Jesus is waiting for you!

Meditation on Jesus in the Eucharist:

Jesus, Come to Me!

Jesus, Come to Me!

I adore Thee in the Holy Eucharist with your Mother Mary!

I adore Thee, I Love You! I Love You! Come to me!

I adore Thee, I love You! I Love You! Come to me!

Pray for me to Mary!

<u>Dad Tip:</u>

Dad's can participate in "Naming their child" by suggesting names to the mother for their baby. Hint: Dad probably has a better chance of getting a name he likes if this is discussed when mom is in a good mood. Mothers should be willing to listen to their "mate's" suggestions. After all naming the child, should be an honor dad gets to help in. One way to settle disagreements – let one of you have first name and second one chooses the middle name. In our house, we decided to choose a name of the child near a feast day in that same month – if we couldn't find one, we liked – we could then search closest month to the baby. For instance, one of our son's names is the month before and month after saints! Our daughter was named after saints in the month of August. Also, if baby was being baptized in following month, then we could choose a saint from that month (in instance of our son). So, I guess make up some rules you agree upon and look for saint names you like under you own rules for instance! We always wanted a saint name. Children needs saints to lookup too. However, St. Gemma when she was born was not named after a particular saint, but her mother had a premonition that her name would be a saint name later. St. Gemma's parents died when she was very young, and she lived with relatives after that time frame. Gemma means Gem for Heaven!!

Doula Tip: Do not get in way of naming children – this is the parents' job. However, if they ask for some resources, you can suggest some saint naming books for instance! If you are a doula, find a few books to share with parents!

Journaling section: Write down your thoughts of the second trimester ending. How do you feel? Are you getting excited to meet your baby?

Chapter 12: Weeks 28-31 – Trimester Third Part One:

"The loveliest masterpiece of the heart of God is the heart of a mother." – St Therese of Lisieux[lxxii] So, St. Therese does have a quote for us mothers! We should remember to unite our hearts with Jesus and Mary each day esp. as we enter the final trimester of this pregnancy! This picture is of St. Zélie, St. Therese's mother. If you want to learn more about this saint of motherhood, go to

https://giveninstitute.com/st-zelie-guerin-martin/

So, now we are in the third trimester. Usually at the beginning of the third trimester or near the end of the second, the doctor may ask you to come in for a glucose test to see if you have any gestational diabetes issues. This means your blood sugar is usually too high. Women who have gestational diabetes tend to have bigger babies and sometimes the babies are harder to birth when bigger – though this is not always the case.[lxxiii] The doctor or midwife usually have you drink a glucose drink that has a lot of sugar in it. There has been new research done now where a mother can do a jellybean study instead of using the glucose drink for this test.[lxxiv] So, if you are a pregnant mother wanting alternatives, we suggest asking your doctor about taking in jellybeans.

Gloria Lemay is a leading midwife who has her own protocols for gestational diabetes – you can read more by going to this **PDF** handout online:

http://consciouswoman.org/wp-content/uploads/gd-handout.pdf[lxxv]

According to Gloria's article women at risk for gestational diabetes include:

Women at risk:

☐ maternal age over 25

☐ obese woman prior to pregnancy

☐ previous birth of baby weighing over 10# at birth

☐ previous unexplained stillbirth at term

☐ family history of diabetes (esp. close relatives who became diabetic at a young age

☐ i.e. juvenile onset diabetes)

previous history of recurrent miscarriages

☐ extremes of heaviness or thinness

☐ history of alcohol abuse

☐ history of anorexia or bulimia

This risk factor screening will only pick up 50% of women who are GD.[lxxvi]

So, a lot of women can fall in this mixed category. However, even though you maybe over 25 years of age and pregnant, does not mean you will have or even get this problem. Diet has a lot to do with getting gestational diabetes in the first place.

One website I like to point people to is this one: https://realfoodforgd.com/

The author Lily Nichols also wrote her first original book titled "Real Food for Gestational Diabetes." She tells women how to reverse this with foods! Also, we believe mindset is also important!

I am currently reading a new book about Brain Power – full title: *Switch On Your Brain: The Key to Peak Happiness, Thinking, and Health* by Dr. Caroline Leaf.

This book shows us that you can control your thoughts and think more positively about any scenario in your life; you may not be able to control others, but you have choice to control your thoughts and actions! It is truly an amazing book. So, let us not think negative of having any kind of disorder; instead we can change our thinking to be more positive.

**Doula Tip:** If a mother is feeling down about a certain diagnosis, have her write down her feelings and thoughts. Then, she may want to read the amazing book above, it shows a 21-day detox on how to get rid of negative thought patterns. At least for now, have her see what is negative thoughts that are bothering her and take out the trash! She should replace it with good images, etc. Read the above book for better details on what to do.

**Dad Tip:**

If mother is feeling down, this might be a good time to go on a "date night" just the two of you. This is also really great for first time pregnancies – however, if you already have a little one or two – find a babysitter – so you can enjoy some alone time with your wife! This is really important for mom to feel loved during her third trimester. She may feel a bit down as she is getting "bigger". Let her feel loved no matter what her shape or size is! Also, invite mom to a funny movie to lift her spirits! Date nights also can be inside the home as well. Perhaps pregnant mama is not wanting to go out, instead you as father can make her a lovely meal and watch a move at your home! Make it a nice "candlelight dinner" and she may just really enjoy remembering this moment of her pregnancy!

Saint of this section: Saint Dymphna[lxxvii]

Saint Dymphna's mother died when she was young. Dymphna has already taken a vow of virginity. Her father wanted to marry his "daughter". How terrible?! His advisors said, "She looks like your wife; take her as your own." Well, Dymphna had to flee Ireland and go to another country for a time. However, she was not able to stay hidden for long. Her father eventually found her and killed her. Since we believe her father was mentally ill – St. Dymphna has been the patroness of mental illness, depression, anxiety, etc.

St. Dymphna, pray for us, who maybe depressed, have pregnancy anxiety, or other problems – lighten our minds to see God's will. Amen.

So, you are probably why am I including St. Dymphna in a pregnancy book? Well, I found this article about St. Dymphna helping a family become pregnant – this is a partial quote from this article:

Once we met Saint Dymphna, everything changed for the good[lxxviii]

By Larry Peterson - published on 07/08/16

A gift of a first-class relic of the teenage saint and the joy it brought

My wife Loretta and I were living in northern New Jersey with our two sons, ages 6 and 2. We wanted more children, and had hoped for a girl, but doctors told Loretta she would never have more kids.

So be it. We had been blessed with two healthy sons.

One day, my mother-in-law was planning to stop at our house for a while, on her way home from visiting St. Benedict's Abbey in Massachusetts.

"Wait until you see what I have," she announced as she breezed through the front door.

She reached into her huge purse and pulled out a beautiful, gold container.

"What is it?" I asked.

"Look inside the glass. It is a first-class relic of St. Dymphna. She is the patron saint of mental and emotional disorders. I asked the priest at St. Benedict if I could borrow this for Marion and Kelly. I'm going to bring it to the hospital and touch it to both of them and ask St. Dymphna for her help."

Marion, our 14-year-old niece, was in the hospital because of her battle with anorexia. Kelly, 16, was facing the same struggle, and the two had become friends in the hospital.

Kelly was down to about 45 pounds and Marion, two years younger, was hovering around 65. My mother-in-law wanted desperately to help these girls who were slowly killing themselves.

My brother-in-law came by later that afternoon and took his mom to visit the girls. She held the relic next to each girl's chest and prayed to St. Dymphna to intercede for them to help them get well. Time would tell how God would respond.

Doctors thought Kelly would not survive but, miraculously, both girls did recover.

St. Dymphna, though, wasn't done bringing surprises to our family, and for me, a bigger one was still to come.

It was about six weeks later. Loretta and I hired a babysitter and headed to the local Italian restaurant. As we ate our lasagna, she (his wife) casually commented, "Oh, by the way, I'm pregnant."

Holding a forkful of lasagna in front of my mouth, I stared at her. A moment or two passed and, as tears ran down her face, she said, "I used the relic."

She had taken the St. Dymphna relic, and holding it to her womb, prayed to the teenage saint. She asked her if she could help her with pregnancy issues. Seven and a half months later, our daughter was born. We named her Mary Dymphna.

The next day, I was beside Loretta in the hospital, as she lay holding Mary Dymphna. An elderly lady delivering newspapers poked her head in the room. "I never speak to patients but for some reason I had to talk to you," she said. "Could you please tell me your baby's name?"

"Sure. It's Mary Dymphna," Loretta answered.

So help me, this old lady started crying. "I knew it, I knew it. St. Dymphna saved my life a long time ago. I knew this baby had something to do with her."

The lady came over, touched Mary's face and gazed at her. She was seeing something we could not in an inexplicable spiritual moment, born of faith. (By Larry Peterson).

More about St. Zélie:

St. Zélie is Saint Therese's mother. She originally wanted to be a religious nun but was turned down. She learned the art of lacemaking. She met Louis Martin on a bridge. He also had been turned down for seminary. Louis after meeting Zélie made immediate arrangements to marry her. It was pretty much a whirlwind romance! There's a lot more to St. Zélie's life in a make-believe diary book that I recently read titled: The Lacemaker, Novel of St. Zélie Martin. Might be a good book to read to learn more about the mother of St. Therese!

Journal about the First part of Third Trimester below:

<u>Chapter Thirteen: Weeks 32-36</u>

St. Therese Quote[lxxix]: *"When something painful or disagreeable happens to me, instead of a melancholy look, I answer with a smile. At first, I did not always succeed, but now it has become a habit which I am glad to have acquired."* I chose this quote because many moms get a lot of looks and questions "When is the baby due?" or "Are you about to pop?" Sometimes as a mother we find these questions disagreeable. However, if we imitate St. Therese then we can turn the question around with a smile!

The baby is growing more now and at 36 weeks some babies are even born "early" and in fact most midwives can deliver a baby 36 weeks and on at a home birth. So, we haven't talked that much about birthplace.

Most women will have a baby in the hospital. However, with covid-stuff, many mothers may be looking at birth centers or home birth now because they want to rule out being exposed to anything at a hospital. Plus, hospitals have really more strict rules now for giving birth. We hope more women will choose birth centers or homebirth now.

Low-risk mothers are kind that will be able to have a birth center or home birth. Low risk usually does not have any previous problems from previous births.

Also, a first-time mom is ideal for homebirth. My first baby was a homebirth. So, we highly suggest a mother to consider midwifery for their first birth! I recently found a pro-life doula association – go to resources in back to find link.

Let's say you are a mother choosing homebirth or birth center birth. You will need to have a birth kit. This is a kit that helps the midwife prepare for your birth. Some items you will use after the birth – things that help heal the perineum for instance – ice packs, etc. There are some places you can buy these birth kits at – so we are going to list them for a resource for you below. Birth Kits usually are around $100 or so for the birth. If you want to do a birth pool, sometimes doulas or midwives will rent you one. A birth pool can be used for labor and then you birth outside the tub, or you can even birth inside the water. One of my births was a waterbirth. It was wonderful. We will put in the resource section about waterbirth as well. For my particular waterbirth, I had been in a car accident 2 days before and it really helped my hurt back when I had the waterbirth! So, waterbirth can really mask a lot of pain – believe me I was in like more pain than usual with that birth! So, I also did a lunge when I got out of the water for a bathroom break and that also helped.

So, here are your resources for this section:

Birth kits: https://www.inhishands.com/birth-kits/

https://www.preciousarrows.com/birthkits_s/28.htm

https://www.everythingbirth.com/Home-Birth-Kits_c_808.html

Waterbirth Kits:

Water birth kit: https://www.inhishands.com/the-water-birth-kit/

https://www.preciousarrows.com/Water_Birth_Kits_s/1.htm

Benefits of Water birth: https://myfamilybirthcenter.com/7-benefits-of-a-water-birth/

Baby Gaga: https://www.babygaga.com/benefits-and-risks-of-water-birth/

Premature birth and Preemie and dealing with NICU[lxxx]

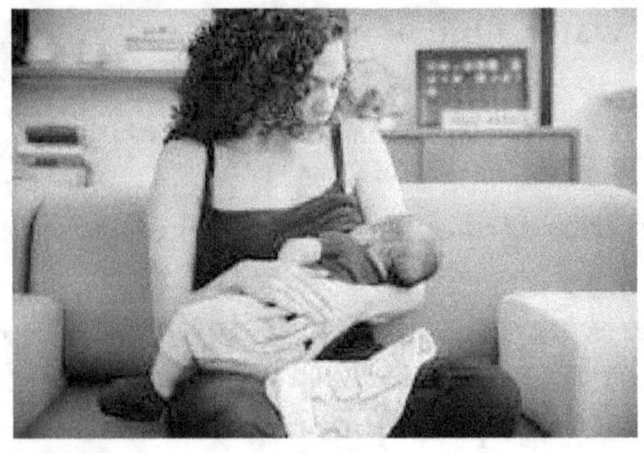

Let's say you are a mom and just happen to give birth early. You may want to study up on what options you have for hospital and the NICU – this is a special unit to help newborn babies that come early. Babies born premature should always have mother's breastmilk – it is best for their systems – they probably have other issues going on and they need mommy milk not formula. Do not agree to formula if you can help it. Either pump your breastmilk esp. a pump from hospital like a Sympathy pump works best. Another option is getting milk bank breastmilk – this milk has a little lower quality because the milk has to be boiled a little bit. However, I suggest it over any formulas. You can even tube feed your breastmilk – so make sure you start pumping from day one! You can teach the baby to suck and eventually baby will be able to suckle at the breast and breastfeed. Another note about NICU, insist on touching your baby daily or even hourly. Some hospitals will have a way for you to hold your baby even if tied up to tubes and such. Premature babies respond better to mother's touch to get well. There may be a place the hospital will let parents stay at for long time for minimal

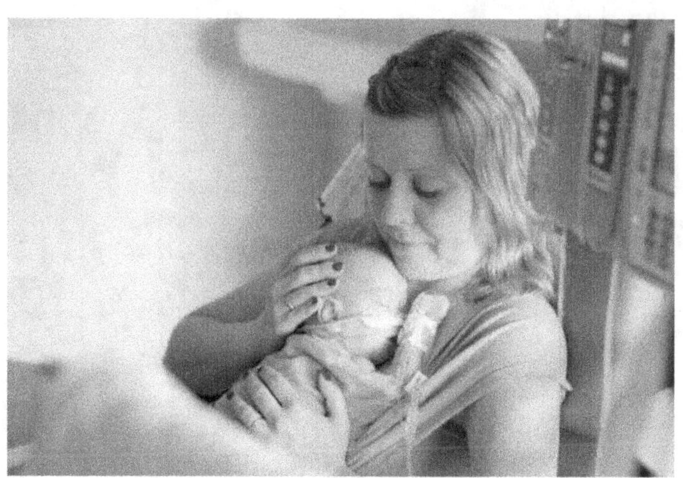

fees – please ask about that. (This is sometimes a Ronald McDonald House for instance).

Kangaroo Care – what is that? This typically means holding the baby up to your skin and having skin-to-skin contact throughout the day. The mother could put the baby in a wrap of some sort to do this. There are various types of baby wraps. Please see later section for related links. The main idea of kangaroo care is for the infant to be swaddled in mother's arms as long as possible after the birth as this reminds the baby of the womb and also helps the baby's body temperature stay more even. Other benefits include knowing the "cues" to when the baby needs to feed or even have a diaper change! We encourage moms to try out holding their baby in a wrap or "kangaroo care". Also, this wrap helps free your hands to do other tasks as needed, though rest is important.

Journaling area for Weeks 32-36[lxxxi]:

<u>Chapter Fourteen: Weeks 37-40 (or till baby arrives):</u>

<u>"Jesus has chosen to show me the only way which leads to the Divine Furnace of love; it is the way of childlike self-surrender, the way of a child who sleeps, afraid of nothing, in its father's arms." – St Therese of Lisieux</u>[lxxxii]

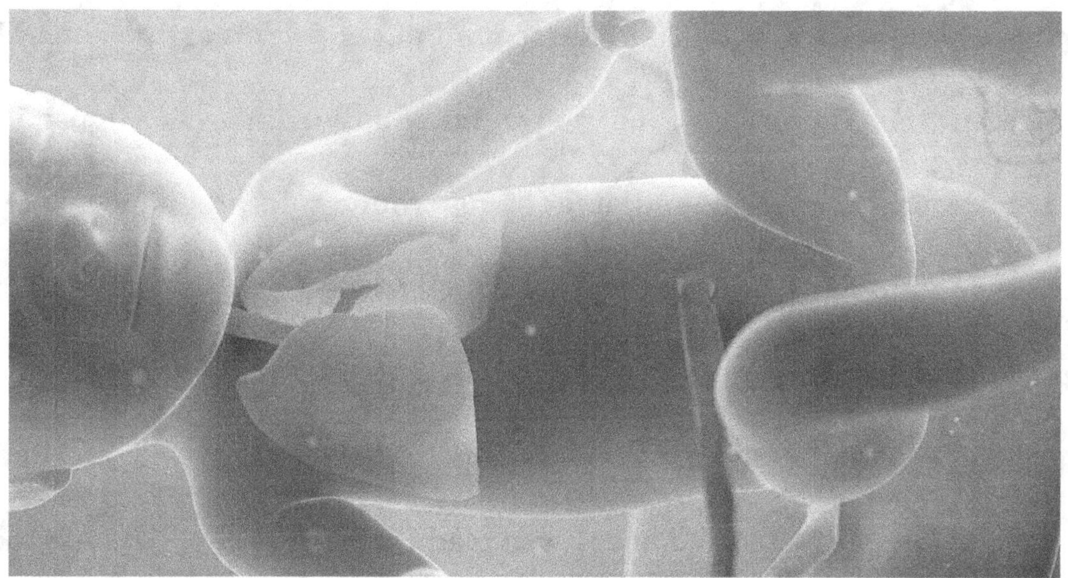

You finally made it – you are now in your last weeks of pregnancy. Did you know that the lungs fully developed usually signal when labor begins? That is why it is important to be patient with the process of waiting for delivery of your baby. Too early and baby's lungs may not be developed as well. Now, we know emergencies happen or other things like pre-eclampsia that may need to have an induction for labor, etc. However, make sure you do all your research before agreeing to an induction procedure. If you are with a home birth midwife, they are most likely to let you wait it out a bit longer. However, even some of those midwives have their "hands tied" so to speak because of various state laws or regulations. So, make sure you understand the restrictions or not. For instance, some home birth midwives may not be able to be your midwife after week 40 (so 41 or longer). You may want to get an ultrasound to verify correct due date. Here's for instance: my daughter's original or so we thought due date was August 5th. However, I was not measuring up that far along around mid-pregnancy. So, we did an ultrasound to figure out a better due date. I was off by 2 weeks – so her due date was moved down to August 23! This gave me "more time" in my pregnancy. Due dates can be off if you did not know your period cycles that well, etc. and that was my case being newly married, etc. I was glad I got a new due date – it meant avoiding an unnecessary induction in the end. However, if you are sure about your due date – you can try castor oil with permission of your midwife or doctor to help induce labor naturally. One can also stimulate the breasts to induce naturally and have sex with your husband (only if your membranes are intact). So, natural induction is another possibility.

Now, let's talk "Bishop's score". What's that? It is a type of score to see how the baby is doing inside of your womb and if an induction is medically necessary –

to time it best so that the baby will not be as distressed. According to one article[lxxxiii] the bishop's score is limited to mothers with placenta previa (where the placenta covers your cervix) or other issues concerning the placenta. So, be careful on how the doctor is using this scoring system. If your pregnancy does not fall under this, then you may need to be patient and ask doctor questions as to why he thinks you need to be induced?!

Here are a few reasons the doctor may want to induce you – from this "Very Well Family" article[lxxxiv]:

"Fetal conditions: If your baby is experiencing certain health conditions, ACOG recommends an early delivery. These include intrauterine growth restriction (IUGR), multiple gestation (if your baby is a twin or triplet), or when there is too little or too much amniotic fluid.

Diabetes (gestational or type I and II): ACOG recommends that pregnant people with gestational diabetes or preexisting diabetes should have labor induced before week 40, especially if they are having trouble managing symptoms or are on medication. Maternal diabetes can put a baby at risk for being overly large, experiencing shoulder injuries during childbirth, or being stillborn.

Hypertension or preeclampsia: Uncontrolled high blood pressure during pregnancy can lead to serious, even fatal complications. It's recommended that pregnant people with severe gestational hypertension or preeclampsia (hypertension with protein in the urine) be induced early.

Placental/Uterine Conditions: Having placenta previa, a previous uterine rupture, or a prior cesarean delivery (c-section) are examples of structural concerns in the womb that might call for an early delivery.

Post-term pregnancy: A baby who has not been born by 42 weeks gestation is at risk for being stillborn, experiencing shoulder injuries or meconium aspiration in the birth canal, or having seizures. For this reason, ACOG says that it's valid to induce birth starting at 41 weeks and recommends inducing birth at 42 weeks. 3

PROM (premature rupture of membranes): If your water breaks prematurely, your doctor may recommend that you deliver as early as 34 weeks."

So, those are some medical reasons for induction. There are various types of induction procedures. Here are some methods (same article as above[lxxxv]):

"Stripping the membranes: During a vaginal exam late in a healthy pregnancy, your doctor or midwife might insert their finger into your cervix and attempt to separate it from the amniotic sac without breaking your water. Less an induction method than a way to coax approaching labor along, membrane stripping can prompt your body to release natural chemicals that soften (or "ripen") your cervix.

Prostaglandins: Another early step in labor induction is the insertion of cervix-softening prostaglandins into your vagina via a gel or suppository.

Pitocin: This is the synthetic version of oxytocin, a natural hormone that starts contractions. Pitocin is given via an IV line, and you'll be monitored to gauge its effectiveness. Dosing can be increased to create a realistic contraction pattern.

Amniotomy: Doctors may break your water artificially after giving you Pitocin if your cervix is thin and dilated. Doctors gently nick the amniotic sac in this painless procedure to create a hole through which fluid can release, stimulating labor.

Foley bulb: This is a catheter with a balloon that is placed through the cervix and expanded. The pressure from the device promotes dilation and contractions."

Have you heard of the **BRAIN** formula? Well, that is a way to analyze your decision-making process for your upcoming birth and any procedures the doctor may want to do.

B = Benefits – what are the benefits of the procedure?

R = Risks – what are the risks to me or the baby?

A = Analyze - Will everyone be **OK** in the long run? Will I be able to have the birth I want? Will I still be able to do this or that? How will the procedure change my birth plan?

I = Intuition – Do I go with my gut or how do I feel about this procedure?

N = Nothing – Can I do nothing for a time (an hour or whatever) and come back to a decision? What would happen if I chose not to do the procedure?

We hope this helps you make better decisions at your birth.

Another thing that can help at a birth, is having a _birth plan or birth wishes_ written down. There are now days "visual birth" plans that have pictures. We suggest having only around 2 pages – keep it short and simple about the birth plan. Since this book is not really about birth plans so to speak – we suggest you look at the book *"The Comfort in Birth Method"* or other books to help you plan your birth better if you need this extra help. Making a birth plan is pretty simple as you should write down what you want at your birth and "not want". Some people call it "birth wishes" as you have to be open to what God wills at your birth and sometimes things do not go according to plan. So, remember God's in control!

Let's say you are all ready for your birth, but you feel like you would like an extra helping hand during the labor time. Great – hire a doula! What's a doula? A doula is a "servant" (Greek) to the mother during her pregnancy and labor. (There are also postpartum doulas too). Finding a doula should not be that hard – but it can be sometimes. We recommend a directory:

http://findacatholicdoula.weebly.com or new one called Life Doulas

http://lifedoulas.weebly.com

If you need any help finding a doula or want a virtual doula, please contact the author at catholicdoulanews@gmail.com for assistance. Thank you.

Doula Interview:

Let's say you want to interview a doula – what questions should you ask her?

1. Are you new or have you been doing this for a while?

2. If newbie (they usually charge less), would you have a backup doula or an experienced doula to talk with during my labor if I had a question, you could not answer?

3. Do you do hospital births, birth center, or home birth? (Depending on where you are giving birth – the conversation may stop here if the doula does not do hospital and you are going to one, etc.)

4. My due date is ---------- do you have availability around that date? If the answer is yes, continue the conversation and if not, you can end your discussion and ask if she can refer you to another doula.

5. Are you Catholic or Christian doula? Yes, this does make a difference. You may want the doula to pray with you during the birth.

6. Are you a sibling doula? This means – the doula may offer services to watch your kids while your husband is your main "doula". However, I do not

recommend doing this with a "stranger". Some doulas do better at doulaing and not babysitting. Technically, that is a glorified name for babysitter. We strongly suggest having a trusted friend babysit during a birth (or better yet grandma!)

7. Do you offer both birth and postpartum services? This could be a win-win to you as a mother because doulas that do both will probably give you a "package deal" and maybe more of a flat rate that you may find more affordable.

8. Do you do payment plans? Most doulas will do that, and they usually have a small deposit required at beginning of their services.

9. How often do I meet with my doula? This varies – but the standard is that you hire the doula at end of 2nd trimester or early third trimester. You meet with her around 2 times before labor begins to get various tips from birth planning to comfort measures.

So, those are a few ideas on what to talk to a doula about. Hopefully, you will find someone that is available around your due date and does your area. Or she may refer you to someone else. Since there are not a lot of *Catholic doulas* out there yet; you may end up with a Christian one.

Let's say you hired a doula – so when do you call your doula when labor begins? I say right away. Most doulas will want to know that you are in labor – and early labor they can even come to your home if pre-arranged to do so. The doula can help you pack your hospital bag (if going there or birth center). The doula can help you labor at home for longer time and offer comfort techniques at your home. Then when it is time to go to the hospital, she can go with you as a guest. (That is what we suggest if hospital has crazy restrictions – she may not be able to go to hospital – so make sure you check – ask how many visitors or guests you can have at your birth?!) If she has to, she can support you virtually for the rest of your labor and birth time and come up to hospital as a visitor shortly after the birth. Make sure you find out what is allowed at your hospital, etc. The covid restrictions vary – make a plan to find out restrictions before the birth.

Doula Tip: Another thing to consider if your mom decides on a homebirth – as a doula you are more likely able to come early to help her and you the doula may even arrive before the midwife. You (as a doula) will have experience usually to know when to call the midwife in for the more intense part of labor. Some moms prefer more hands-off approach which is another beautiful way of having labor – she may only want the doula there to support her more emotionally. Remember to respect the mother's wishes. If she has a "birth plan" or "birth wishes" written down, make sure you have a copy to know what she wants as her doula. (End of Doula tip).

Home birth and birth center births should be less restrictive on what you can do or not do depending on the midwife. Note: There are two types of midwives. "Med-wives" are midwives who want to follow more like the medical system of thinking. Traditional midwives are more likely to be open to nature's way and letting birth happen on its own.

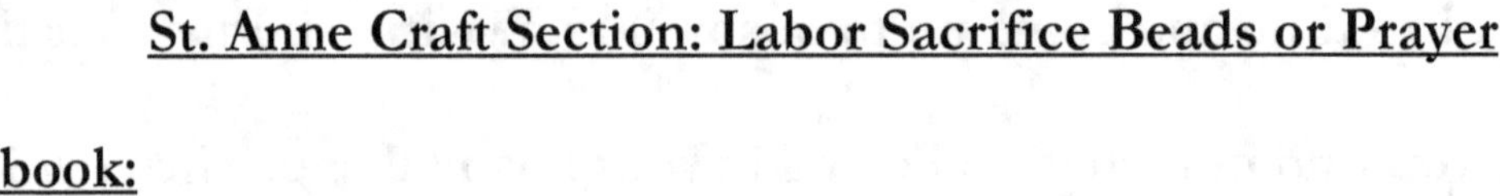

St. Anne Craft Section: Labor Sacrifice Beads or Prayer book:

This idea has come to me from my personal doula clients. A mother who is Catholic may like to ask her friends to pray for their intentions during labor. So, this mother would write down her friends' prayers intentions in a book or notebook or print them out and take with her during labor time. During labor, she would read off or have her husband or doula read off intentions during labor. She may do this during early labor or mid-labor – probably will not have the "concentration" at the end of labor – so try to remember to do this during early labor if you want to imitate this idea. Even if you do not read off all intentions –

taking the book with you and praying for "all intentions" in the book will suffice! You may find this a helpful way to concentrate on something during early or mid-labor time.

A craft idea you can make a string of sacrifice beads to use during labor. St. Therese as a child would have a string of beads in her pocket and would pull one down each time, she offered a "sacrifice" to Jesus.

<u>Instructions on How to Make Sacrifice Beads from Catholic Icing</u>[lxxxvi]

Supplies Needed to Make Sacrifice Beads

3 feet of silk cord (The string must fit through the bead twice. Avoid the plastic "gimp" string and definitely do not use anything elastic. If you use yarn, you'll want to put a piece of clear tape round each end to keep the yard from unraveling and make the stringing easier for children if doing with family members.)

A key ring (or St. Therese medal), pony beads (this is a good kind of bead to use because you need a bead with a large hole), crucifix, clear fingernail polish.

How To Make Sacrifice Beads

You're going to start with your St. Therese medal or your key ring. Find the middle of your string and put it through the end of your St. Therese medal or key ring. This will make a loop with the middle of the string. Take the 2 ends of your string and put them through the loop. Pull the 2 ends of the string tight, and it will attach the string to your St. Therese medal or key ring, leaving 2 strings dangling down. You can lay out 10 pony beads and decide the order you want to string them in. I am going to make a pattern with pink, purple, and white beads. Take your first pony bead, and put one string through one side, and one string through the other side. Pull both ends of the string and the pony bead will start sliding up towards your medal. Keep pulling the 2 strings in opposite directions until your bead goes all the way up to the top. Now do the same to another bead- 1 string going in each side of the bead. Keep repeating this step until you have 10 beads on your string. Then leave a space and tie a knot by wrapping the string around your fingers and putting the ends of the string through the hole. This knot needs to be big enough to hold the pony bead in place, so make a double knot if you need to. Please see this link if you want full pictures of how to make this:

https://www.catholicicing.com/make-your-own-sacrifice-beads/

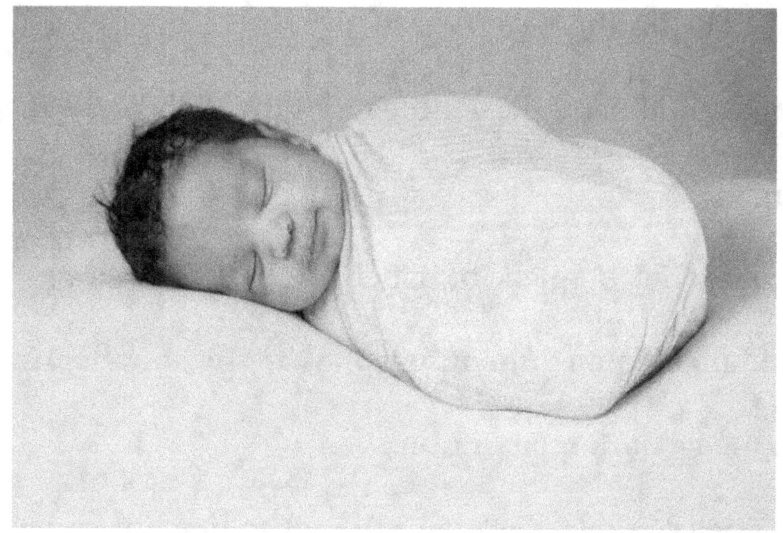

Congratulations – your baby has arrived!! Now, our next chapter or two we will talk about breastfeeding your newborn since we think that information is lacking in a lot of pregnancy manuals.

Doula Tip: If you are a doula for a mother, make sure to give her a short thank you card for allowing you to be her doula for her birth!

Dad Tip: We know mom is in the limelight – however, enjoy snuggling with the newborn and get some good pictures of baby! Make sure you are in one too!

We will leave some space on the page below for your journaling section. Enjoy your precious new baby.[lxxxvii]

Chapter 15: Labor Tips for Christian or Catholic Mothers:

This is one area that mothers want more information about. So, I hope this section is helpful.

Tips for Laboring as a Catholic Mother:

1. **Offer it up!** I know easier said than done. Think about the Holy Souls in Purgatory while you are in labor.

2. **Write down intentions** of friends on piece of paper and pray for friends during labor time. We mentioned making an "intention" book in the above crafts – so now you can put that book to use during labor time.

3. <u>Pray for strength!</u> That one is simple – ask your friends to pray for you and pray a Rosary at least in early labor time.

<u>Prayer for Labor Time:</u>

Oh, Jesus and Mary help me walk the journey of labor time.

I wish my labor and birth to be sublime.

Teach me the ways of your will...

So, my heart will be filled...

When my baby arrives in my arms

May the baby stay away from harms! Amen.

4. Comfort tips: There's a lot of things a mother can do for natural labor to take place – she can move around, use a birth ball, use a Mexican Rebozo shawl, and more. Learning about the rebozo may help and make the difference in labor time. Mexican rebozo shawl classes are online and available at http://rebozo.weebly.com – to get more information. These rebozo classes are for parents and doulas.

5. Letting go of fears of labor and pain: This is a short exercise you can try to get rid of fears of labor: Write down what fears you have about labor – let's say you don't like hospitals. Then put this piece of paper into a place that you can burn it up or tear it up and throw it away. Then sit down quietly in a quiet place and ask God to let you "let go of this fear" that you just tore up or burned! Now, ask God for some positive idea to help you deal with this – it could be anything you think about. Write this new thought down – like "I'll remember that this is temporary" or "I'll bring essential oils to diffuse during labor." Whatever tickles your fancy. And don't worry if you really do it or not – anything goes for this. Writing things

down is powerful. And remember it is ok to release tears, frustration, etc. If your doula is working with you, she can be a "shoulder to cry on" so to speak.

6. Hire that doula: So, perhaps you have the funds to hire a doula for your upcoming birth. Who do you hire? There are some finder sites for finding Christian or Catholic doulas (http://findacatholicdoula.weebly.com). I would also ask around locally as there are a lot of doulas that can be in your community and perhaps, they are not quite advertising they are Catholic or Christian – word of mouth is a good way to find a doula. After you find and hire your doula, make sure you listen well to what she teaches. Remember to be respectful of her role. The doula usually wants you to be happy about your outcome of your birth. Remember to ask her to work with your husband/partner if they are coming to the birth too.

7. Get dad to help: Dads/partners are great helpers for birth. Remember to include them in childbirth classes. If you are looking for an online class – see resources for some information. Local classes are great too – however, we notice that a lot of regular classes do tend to go towards a more medical mindset and epidural mindset. So, be careful of which childbirth classes you attend. Also, there's nothing wrong with doing more than one style of class – perhaps you

would benefit from a Catholic or Christian one and local class. Ask for scholarship for the online class if possible (esp. if taking 2 classes)!

8. <u>Welcome your baby with gentleness:</u> Welcoming your baby with gentleness – remember to ask for delayed cord clamping at birth, less baby interventions such as no shots at birth (this kind of stuff can be decided later) and wait on patting down the baby. Here's an article about that to read more: https://birthweeklynews.wordpress.com/2014/02/03/newborns-no-hatting-patting-chatting/ **Reprinting with permission from author below:**

Yes, I have heard of this, "No hatting, patting, chatting." Who has coined this term? Carla Hartley of www.trustbirth.com

So, what does this mean? I can't get a cute baby hat for my baby? Well, for immediately after birth, the baby does not need a silly stripped or "cute" hat. In fact according to some research (see resources), the idea of hat does not make sense. The mama needs to smell that baby scent right after birth. It actually helps the third stage of labor. What third stage? Many moms, parents, and whoever forget that the placenta is the actual third stage of delivery. So, the mom needs to smell that wonderful new baby scent and she cannot do so if the baby's head is covered.

So, what if the baby gets cold? No chance as long as the baby is skin to skin immediately after birth and has blankets on top of him, then the baby is going to be just fine without the hat. In fact he might get over heated with a hat on. Labor and delivery are a lot of work, the baby's circulation might not work so great with a hat on his head. So, take the stupid hat off. And if a nurse tries to put it on again, just continue to take it off! Tell her to throw the thing away! OK, so what about the no patting? What does this mean? Sometimes a doctor likes to pat the baby a lot to get fluids and stuff like that out of the poor kid or to get him breathing better. But, really, is it necessary? Not really. Unless the baby has a real hard time breathing, those extra pats and rubs are not necessary. Just give the baby to mom or let dad catch the baby even and then hand baby to mom. That's all the patting that is needed. No need to clean the baby up right away. All that vermix is also good for the baby. Do not rub it off!

So, what about no chatting? Isn't it okay to celebrate a little bit–we have a baby! Break out the champagne! Well, it is better for mom and baby after all that work of labor just to have some quiet time to get to know each other. Let mom deliver the placenta quietly and try not to talk too much. Let mom adore her little baby in her arms after delivery. Let dad cut the cord quietly (after it stops pulsating—or even after the placenta is delivered). (Or just have a lotus birth and let the cord fall off naturally later). It is quiet time now, mom and baby have been through a lot–let them rest for a few hours. Visitors can stop by later. It is best for mom and baby to have quiet time to learn how to breastfeed and get to know each other. The doula can even leave now that quiet time is here. She can always return later if mom needs extra support breastfeeding, etc. (Doula is probably ready for a break too!)

So, let's remember these items–we should encourage moms to stop and listen to their bodies and remember–"no hatting, patting, and chatting." Sounds good to me! (End of No Hatting, Patting Article)[lxxxviii]

Extra Section Birth Stories section:

This first one is by Cayla Mello:

It was my first pregnancy. I was at my 40 week check up with my **OBGYN**, one day after my son's due date. "How do you feel?" she asked.

"Tired and ready to have my body back so I can meet this baby," I replied.

"Have you had any contractions?" she asked as I laid down on the bed.

"No," I said.

As she measured my belly, she said, "you're having one right now."

I said, "oh I have a lot of those. But they can't be contractions because they don't hurt like everything says they will hurt. It's just a Braxton-hicks."

My abdomen relaxed again. She started checking the baby's heart beat. She found it and then promptly lost it as my abdomen got rock hard again. "You're having another," she said. "I'm going to check your cervix and we'll see about your so called 'Braxton-hicks'."

I winced as she checked inside me. She removed her hand, looked me in the eye, and said, "you are 6cm. Your contractions are just over a minute apart. You are in labor right now. You need to go to the hospital. I'll meet you up there. You're having a baby today!"

"No, I can't, that can't be right..."

"And, by the way your powerful contractions are affecting you, I'd say you could do it all naturally if you want."

That was a boost of confidence. My husband had suggested I not receive anything for the pain. "It's better for the baby," he said. "He'll come out alert and ready to meet us with no drugs in his little body to harm him."

I, however, was torn. I was terrified of the pain surely to come. My husband didn't have to birth a baby, I did. Even though I was scared of what was coming, I was more scared of a needle in my spine. My fear of needles in my spine and my doctors encouraging words strengthen and finalized my will. I was going to have this baby and it was going to be a natural birth.

I thanked my **OBGYN** and went home. I called my husband and told him the news. I finished packing our bag and we left for the hospital.

As I checked into the hospital, I could tell the receptionist did not think I should be there, "are you sure you want to check in? They'll just send you home," she told us. "You'd know if you were in labor. That smile would be wiped right off your face," she assured me.

"My doctor asked me to come."

"All right, have a seat in that wheelchair and go on up."

"Thank you, but I can walk."

"No, it's company policy, have a seat. In the elevator," she pointed, "up two floors, it's to the right."

The nurse smiled as I was wheeled into the labor and delivery room. "It's not often we see patients in such light moods," she said. I told my tale, and she checked my cervix and was astounded that yes indeed I was 6cm, "but you sure don't look it. You look like you're ready for a stroll downtown."

"So, what do we do now?" I asked.

"Well, I'm going to hook you up to the equipment so we can hear baby's heartbeat, get an IV into you, and then we wait."

"Oh, I don't want an IV; I'm going to have a natural birth."

"It's just a mandatory precaution. We want you to be ready for anything."

When she left, I felt my hard belly and smiled.

My doctor came in about 45 min later. Again she checks my cervix and it had not dilated any further. She told me she was going to pop my water to stimulate the progress. I agreed.

There was a rush of warm liquid and a few minutes later -an extremely intense contraction. I gripped my husband's hand and moaned. "Keep breathing," he encouraged.

45 seconds later, another hard contraction came. It was so long and hard I couldn't speak. The nurse came in and I tried to smile at her. "Now you look like you're in labor," she smiled back.

20 min later the contractions were so fierce I was nauseous. I told my husband I had to go to the bathroom. I expelled all that was in me from both ends as another contraction racked my body.

The doctor came in and saw I was throwing up. She asked the nurse to help me back to the bed and they gave me a bed pan. "You must be very close," my OBGYN said, "we don't need a baby coming on the bathroom floor." She rechecked my cervix and I doubled over in pain as my contraction impeded her willed and experienced hand. "9cm," she said. "I'll be back in an hour or so. You are doing great!"

As soon as she left, I knew there was no time. The most extreme contraction hit, and I yelled with it. It was nearly a minute long and there was only 30 seconds rest before the next one hit. It was even worse. My doctor, who hadn't left after all, walked back in the room took one look, smiled, and said, "are you ready to push?"

10 seconds later I was filled with the instinct to push hard. I screamed with the contraction and felt a small relief as my baby's head was released from the hold my body had on him. "Keep breathing," my doctor told me as my hands and face were locked and I couldn't move them. "We need to get him out with the next contraction, the cord is wrapped around his neck, and he is turning blue."

When the next one hit, I pushed with all my might, my body released him, and flooded with relief. The nurse asked my husband to hold an oxygen mask over my face. I breathed deeply and movement returned to my hands and face. My face tingled and my hands shook violently. I watched as they put my son on a cart, and he turned his head and looked at me as they wheeled him to the other side of the room. I knew he would be fine.

When they were done with the initial tests, they brought him to me and asked his name. "Matias," my husband said as I tried to feed him for the first time with shaky hands. "Take deep breaths," my doctor remind me. "You did so well!"

"I've never seen a natural birth. It was powerful. You are so strong," added my nurse. I held my baby and smiled. I did it. I was proud of myself.

After the birth, because I had lost so much blood and torn so badly (my husband said it looked like raw hamburger) it took me a week before I could walk on my own and two weeks before I could walk comfortably. The doctor thought it was because I went from 6cm to 10cm in 45 minutes and there was just no time for my body to adjust. It went into shock and took longer to heal because of it.

I didn't mind though. I had a precious baby in my arms, and it felt so good.

<u>Written by Cayla Mello</u>

<u>**Birth Story 2 – A Waterbirth Story by C.R.**</u>

My birth story starts a couple of days before my baby's birth. I was driving home, and we have an alley way in back of our home. So, I drove down the alley way and this stupid person coming out clipped and T-boned my car as I was going down. I even tried to avoid him, but he still hit my car. I was in terrible pain that evening. I called my midwife and she kind of gave me a couple of options – stay at home and try to take care of the pain or go to the ER. I was afraid that if I went to the ER, they might induce my labor and birth. So, I decided to stay home and endure the pain of the accident. I remembered these words of St. Therese: "My whole strength lies in prayer and sacrifice; these are my invincible arms; they can move hearts far better than words." Things calmed down and I was able to wait for real labor.

The real labor came around 2 am in the morning and had some contractions. I think I was able to go back to sleep for a little bit. I woke up again in early morning and decided that we needed to leave soon to get to the birth center. My husband gathered up our 2 other children and dropped them off at pre-arranged babysitter's house and we drove over to the birth center a few miles from our home.

At the birth center, I was first hooked up to an IV since I had GBS Positive –
I got IV antibiotics. We also had planned a water birth, so the birth center had set
up the tub for me while I was getting the IV. My doula arrived at the birth center
as well with the midwife.

After the IV was out, I was able to get into he water tub for laboring in. My
back was still hurting some from the car accident, but once I was in the water
almost all pain was gone! I labored for a time but felt a little stuck. I got out to use
the restroom and my midwife suggested some lunges to help baby get unstuck
and down the canal. So, I tried that, and it seemed to help. I got back into the
water, and I felt ready to push. My doula suggested "blowing technique" in
between contractions (or pressure waves) and I did that. This "blowing
technique" is an Ina May move. It really helped. I was able to push out baby's
head after one contraction and then push out the rest of baby's body on second
contraction. I did not know the gender of our child. My husband was there and

announced, "It's a boy!" as I picked him out of the water and started to nurse him

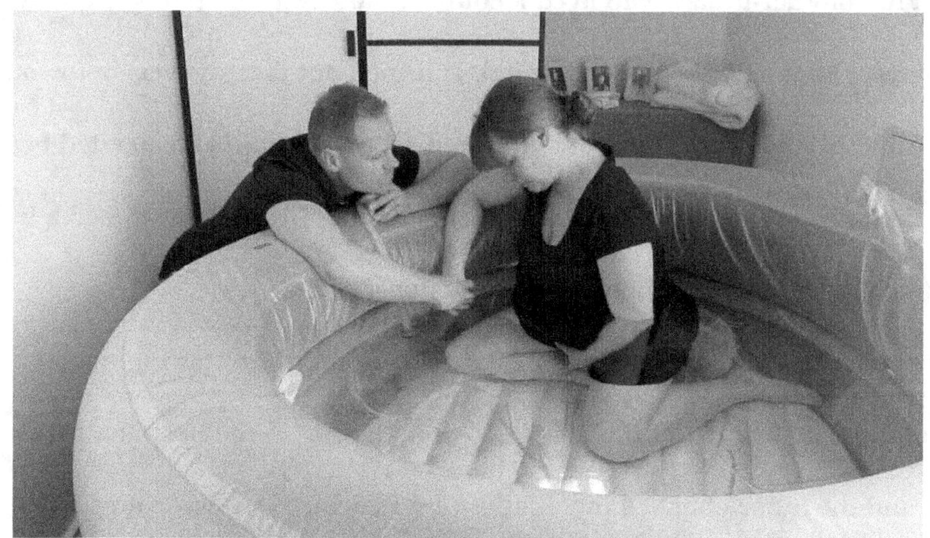

pretty much right away. We weighed him in at 8 lbs. 3 oz. that was a "big baby" for me as I am a tiny person! We were ecstatic!

He also breastfed really well too!

By C.R.^{lxxxix}

Birth Stories by Amy Lynch (1st one – 3rd one in our series):

As I was nearing my due date with my third baby, I had a mental list of things that I wanted to get done before the baby arrived. My husband and I already had 2 young boys and now we were expecting again, but we didn't know if the baby would be a boy or girl. I had started my maternity leave from work, so I had time to finish getting things ready in our new house. On an afternoon in early November, just two days before my official "due date", I finally finished all the items on my "to do" list. I sat down at the dining room table to rest for a few moments. Did I feel a contraction?

I started having mild contractions late that afternoon, they started off about ten minutes apart. We called my mother-in-law who lived a couple hours away, so that she could come stay with our two boys while we went to the hospital. It turned out that she was in town for a work meeting, so she would be able to come right over when ever we thought we needed her. By 11:30pm, I knew that this was definitely labor and not just Braxton Hicks. We watched a little TV and then tried to get some rest. I slept in between contractions.

At 4:00am my contractions were coming every 4-5 minutes and starting to last longer, so we called the doctor and headed to the hospital. After arriving at the hospital, I was brought to a triage room and the nurse checked my dilation, I was 5cm. That was enough to keep me and the hospital and not send me back home! By the time they got me settled in my own room, started an IV, hooked up the fetal monitor, etc., I was getting very uncomfortable. The nurses were asking me questions about my medical history, but I was getting irritated because my contractions were getting much more intense. My doctor wasn't at the hospital, so the nurse wanted to check my cervix again to see if things were progressing faster than anticipated. It was less than an hour since she had just checked, but I was already 7 cm.

I got up to use the bathroom and to move around a little bit, but my contractions were getting closer, longer, doubling up, and more intense. I started to feel like pushing! The nurse wanted to check me again to before they could give me the go ahead to push. Also, they wanted to call my doctor to see how far away he was, as he hadn't arrived at the hospital yet. It turns out that I was almost completely dilated, my cervix had just a "lip" remaining. The nurse told me not to push, and that she was calling the doctor again. He was five minutes away. The nurse kept telling me not to push. I told her that I couldn't wait, so I just did little pushes. Thankfully, I only had one more contraction before my doctor arrived.

As soon as he walked in the door, I pulled my legs up and started pushing. Again, the nurse was telling me to wait because she wanted to check my cervix one last time. As, she did my water broke and sprayed everywhere. My doctor respected my wishes to be hands off. He let me push, while he just stood back. I felt like was doing well, sitting in bed pushing, but the nurses put the head of the bed down, so I was more in a reclined position. It felt awkward and made it more difficult for me to feel like I was pushing effectively, but they told me that that was better, so they just left it down.

It seemed as though I had one long contraction so I just kept pushing until my baby was born at 6:29am, just two hours after we arrived at the hospital. My husband said, "It's another boy!" We were so happy! I couldn't believe that we had another boy. Another boy! We named him Lucca Gabriel. He was 8lbs 10oz.

While every birth is an amazing and special experience. I did feel as though this labor was interrupted by frequent cervical checks, being told not to push when my body wanted to do otherwise, and then not being able to push in the position that felt comfortable to me. I did really like my doctor and he was respectful of my wishes. However, the nursing staff, was just used to their routine of care, so that's what I received even though it was frustrating to me. For my subsequent pregnancy, my husband and I sought care from a Certified Nurse-Midwife and had our baby at a free-standing birth center.

<u>Second Birth Story by Amy Lynch and 4th birth story of our series:</u>

My labor started on my youngest son's birthday, I woke up around 2:30am with some contractions, that were strong enough to wake me up, yet not too uncomfortable either. I was thinking to myself that we might have two children with the same birthday. I continued to have contractions throughout the day, they came every 20-30 minutes, and again, were strong enough that I knew they were labor contractions, but I was still able to go for a walk, do some last minute cleaning around the house, and rest.

In the evening, after our older children went to bed my contractions started to get a little bit closer together, 10-20 minutes between them. I went to bed early because I was starting to get uncomfortable and had to actively try to relax with them. I was able to sleep a little bit, but every contraction woke me up. Rather than get closer together my contractions just seemed to get longer, lasting from 1.5-2.5 minutes each. Around 1am I was starting to get very uncomfortable (we turned the clocks back that night, so I'm a little confused about what time it really was), my contractions were variable from 7-10 minutes apart, but long and hard. They started to double peak or come 2 in a row without any break in between them. I was starting to feel more pressure in my pelvis, so we called our midwife and left for the birthing center.

On our way to the birthing center (about a 20-minute drive) I only had one contraction. I was a little afraid that we would get there, and I would only be 3cm dilated, but something just told me it was time to go.

Once we arrived, I was able to relax knowing that I was in the place where I would give birth. The lights were low, and it was quiet. My midwife told me that I was 9cm dilated!! I just couldn't believe it. I got into the birthing pool and the warm water felt amazing. I was wishing that we had come sooner so that I could have relaxed in the water with some of the hard contractions I was having at home. My body was able to just float in the water, and that made relaxing all my muscles to just let my uterus work, much easier. My contractions, however, were still very intense. Soon after getting in the water I felt like I needed to bear down. I started slowly with some small pushes, grunting through the contractions, however that "urge to push" just took over. I had to push much harder to relieve the intensity of the contraction. It wasn't very long before I could feel my baby moving down the birth canal, I remembered this feeling from my other births and knew that it wouldn't be long before my baby was here.

My husband, midwife and nurse were present in the room. I pushed hard with my contractions and suddenly felt my baby's head crowning. I had a moment of fear, I just wanted to stop because everything was so intense, but I knew I had to do it, I had to give that final push and birth my baby. I reached down into the water and felt the baby's head about to emerge and my body pushed again, and my baby's head was born. There was one more push and my baby was here at last, at 2:38am (the day after contractions had started). I don't remember my midwife saying much to me during this time, but I knew that she was there and had confidence in me. She didn't tell me what to do or how to do it, but instead let me push the way my body needed to in order to birth my precious baby.[xc]

My husband looked to see if we had a boy or girl and announced that *we had a girl.* There were tears all around the room. We were only at the birth center for about 45 minutes before she was born! Siena Joslyn was born November 7, 2010 at 2:38am. She weighed 6lb 14.5oz and was 18.5 inches long.

We were so happy to have had a birth in an environment that supported us, gave us confidence, and allowed us to go home that same morning. We were able to have breakfast as a family with our older children, and then get some rest in our own bed. This experience was everything that I had been wanting with my hospital births, I was just looking in the wrong place. The births of my older children are precious memories that I will never forget, but this birth was just the icing on the cake.

<u>Room to Write your own birth story below:</u>

Chapter 16: Breastfeeding 101:

"Remember that nothing is small in the eyes of God. Do all that you do with love." – St Therese of Lisieux.[xci] In this quote summarizes most of St. Therese's teachings – remember to breastfeed with love of your child!

Positive Breastfeeding Story by Cayla Mello:

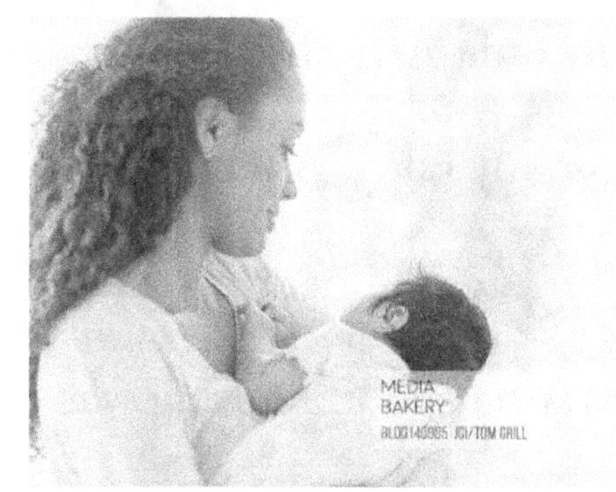

"I was a lucky one. My four children all seemed to know exactly what they were doing when it came to breastfeeding. They opened their mouths wide and took it all in, latched and looked me in the eye. I always made sure to be off my phone while breastfeeding. It is such a precious time, and I didn't want to waste it. I wanted to be available to that beautiful bundle in my arms. If I did do something other than sing or rub my little one, I would read a book out loud to them. A book I was interested in, not a baby book or anything. They heard my voice and became familiar with words. My children always had an enormous vocabulary when they started talking. I credit it to always reading to them all levels of books.

I was never big on routines. I fed my babies when they were hungry and allowed them to sleep when they were tired. I was blessed to be able to do this as I was a stay-at-home mom thanks to the work of my husband at the time.

I did end up having one difficulty with breastfeeding. It was a hot summer, and we had no air-conditioning in the house. My second child was under a month old. I just didn't feel my milk coming out as it normally did. I felt him pulling and pulling and trying to satiate himself with little help from my body. After a few feedings like this, I was worried. I called la leche league and told her my concerns. She assured me it was just my milk coming in and a new baby and nothing was wrong. I stressed that my milk had already come in and it didn't feel right. She wasn't really sure what to say. Later that day I realized I was thirsty. I wondered when the last time I had really drank water. At that point, it all made sense. I had lost my water bottle which I always kept with me for frequent drinks. With it gone, I had not kept myself hydrated. Immediately I drank many cups of water and the next time my baby was at my breast; he was able to drink his fill. Take care of yourself so your body can take care of your little one."

So, for some breastfeeding can be easy as one, two, three and it can come naturally. However, for some moms a little more "training" or "help" is needed.

Another breastfeeding story – by the author:

My own first-time experience, my daughter had a hard time latching on for some reason. She would latch on and then nip or bite me it seemed. I was so sore after the first 2 weeks of breastfeeding, that I almost gave up completely. My midwife suggested that I probably was not making enough milk, so I agreed to doing formula and pumping my milk too. So, I would be up every 2 hours at night pumping my milk, feeding her formula and my breastmilk too. She seemed happier after a couple of weeks or so and finally started sleeping longer at night! I felt like a zombie for at least a month before I got into the routine right. LOL. Anyway, so some babies may need formula or breast pumping to get them fed and full. Do not feel like a failure because you had to use formula. I will never judge a mother again about bringing a bottle to Mass – that mom maybe struggling with breastfeeding, and she may have pumped her milk for Mass. My next two children seemed to breastfeed pretty well; however, my first son startled easily at noise, so I had to always nurse him in a quiet space. The second son didn't care – he would nurse anywhere – he just didn't like covers that much. LOL. My last son I had to do full time pumping with him! So, each child is special and has their own abilities on nursing plus their own nursing styles!

Nursing or Breastfeeding Styles:

The quiet one – this child has to have no noise in order to breastfeed well. This child will like a dark place to breastfeed in. So, though some "cry rooms" are great for babies – if there are noisy children in them – then this is not a good place when at Mass. The best place at Mass might be more in back of church or a confessional not in use!! I read one lady would go inside the confessional and breastfeed during Mass. I thought that was kind of unique – so good idea if one is available.

The fussy nurser – this child will be a bit fussy when nursing or breastfeeding. They may latch on and off quite often before getting in a rhythm. The best thing to do is be patient with a fussy nurser – because once they get into the rhythm they will be fed and full. So, try starting out in a quiet space and the baby may like that better.

The eat anywhere baby – this child loves to just nurse and he/she does not care where. They do not like being covered up sometimes – so you may want to wear a top that is a nursing style top or dress that way you can kind of "cover naturally" without covering the baby's head. This baby is a champion in any noise and probably will not mind the cry room noises as much.

The sleep nurser – this baby wants to sleep more than nurse. So, you may have to wake him/her up before nursing and encourage him/her to breastfeed. You may need to put some of your breastmilk on your nipple and this may help the baby wake up and eat more. This baby probably will also do fine in a cry room area.

If you are looking for an educator program go to www.mommylatch.com

<u>Breastfeeding Tips 101:</u>

1. Breastfeeding should not hurt – if it does. Stop. Re-Access the baby's latching. The baby's mouth should include part of the areola area of the breast – not just the nipple.

2. Take breaks and relax. Make sure you are relaxed while nursing.

3. Eat and drink while nursing. It is ok to have a snack while nursing your baby and be well hydrated.

4. Take a breastfeeding class before baby arrives. Knowing how to breastfeed is an "art of learning" not just something that always comes easy. Some mothers have to work at breastfeeding more than others. So, be prepared!

5. Ask for help – if your baby is not latching right or you feel sore. Then reach out to a breastfeeding specialist or friend.

6. Listen to music to relax. Music can help you unwind more and get the milk flowing!

7. Take some herbs to help with breastfeeding – Moringa and Fenugreek come to mind.

8. Remember breastfeeding is the baby learning as well!

9. Don't forget tongue-ties – you may need to ask the doctor if this is an issue.

Journaling space:

Bonus Section:

<u>Section A: Churching of Women:</u>

Here's information about this ceremony[xcii]:

I have been researching the ritual titled "Churching of Women". This is an old forgotten Catholic Church ritual for women after giving birth that is a special blessing just for the mother after childbirth.

In the old days, this blessing was given around 40 days after birth because women would actually have a "lying in" period where they would rest and have relatives help take care of them. This idea of having a real "postpartum lying-in" is coming back now.

So, many women would not even be able to attend the baptism of their child - the godparents would be there with the father. The mother is excused from church or attendance at Mass for around 4-6 weeks after the birth of the baby. So, when the mother came to Church for the first time - she would request the "Churching of Women" ceremony as a special blessing for her return to Mass and Sacraments, etc.

This is not the same thing as the Jewish ceremony who considered women "unclean" till they went through a cleanings ritual after birth. Our Blessed Lady did this to show her humility and in fact she is known in Ecuador as a special title: Our Lady of Good Event of the Purification (also known in USA as Our Lady of Good Success).

Anyway, the Churching of Women might be more like an "imitation" of this original Jewish ritual - but it is not the same thing.

Psalm 23 is recited for part of the ritual. Psalm 23

P: The Lord's are the earth and its fullness; * the world and those who dwell in it. All: For He founded it upon the seas * and established it upon the rivers.

P: Who can ascend the mountain of the Lord?

* or who may stand in His holy place?

All: He whose hands are sinless, whose heart is clean, who desires not what is vain, * nor swears deceitfully to his neighbor.

P: He shall receive a blessing from the Lord, * a reward from God, his Savior.

All: Such is the race that seeks for Him, * that seeks the face of the God of Jacob.

P: Lift up, O gates, your lintels; reach up, your ancient portals, * that the king of glory may come in!

All: "Who is this king of glory?" * "The Lord, strong and mighty, the Lord, mighty in battle."

P: Lift up, O gates, your lintels; reach up, you ancient portals, * that the king of glory may come in!

All: "Who is this king of glory?" * "The Lord of hosts; He is the king of glory."

P: Glory be to the Father. All: As it was in the beginning. Amen.

I have done some fuller research and found variations on a theme you might say - there are more than one ceremony listed online. Some have Latin and

English in them - so you can read the ritual in English. The links below have some fuller information or articles about the ritual.

Basically, the mother will go to the vestibule doors and the priest will then come to let her into the Church. She may be given a candle to hold and light during the ceremony. Then they will proceed to the altar rail (probably the Marian side) to recite the prayers from the ritual. The priest will then bless the mother with holy water at the end of the ceremony.

We suggest that mothers request the ceremony before the birth of the baby; and set up a time to do the ceremony. Note: Now days many women will go to the baptism ceremony of their babies now. I went to all my children's baptism ceremonies. One thing you can probably do is request this little "Churching ceremony" to be done either BEFORE the baptism - maybe if baptism for instance is being done after a Mass - perhaps the Churching of Women ceremony can be done for the mother BEFORE the Mass - she could arrive a little bit earlier and have it done before the Mass.

Another idea is the Churching ceremony is done immediately after the baptism - in that case the mother does not need to go back to the vestibule door - she can kneel at the altar rail to receive the special ceremonial blessing!

I am wondering though if a mother who never received this blessing could receive it years after a birth? I would probably ask a priest - I bet a traditional one may not mind offering it. In fact, my plan is to ask a pastor or priest to do this for me. And I'll let you know my results later of a yes or no answer!

So, a mother should request this and if she has forgotten to ask before baby's birth; then she should do so immediately after the birth. By the way, the ceremony can be done sooner than 4-6 weeks - this is just a suggested time frame. Many mothers get the baby baptized sooner - so it would be appropriate to do it around the baptismal time if desired.

I hope these resources below will help you explore this more!

https://www.showerofrosesblog.com/2017/07/churching-of-women.html

https://catholicsaints.info/externals-of-the-catholic-church-the-churching-of-women/

https://orthochristian.com/59516.html (yes, I know this is an Orthodox link - but has some info in it).

https://www.churchpop.com/2016/12/30/the-forgotten-tradition-of-churching-an-ancient-post-partum-blessing/

Ceremonial words:

https://latinmassbaptism.com/files/Churching_of_Women_LatinEnglish.pdf

https://catholicstand.com/churching-women-postpartum-support-catholic-style/ https://latinmassbaptism.com/churching-of-women/

Bonus Section B: Baptism and Choosing godparents!

"Amen, amen I say to thee unless a man be born again of water and the Holy Ghost, he cannot enter into the kingdom of God." John 3:1-21. The story of Nicodemus is an important one to re-read. So, the Sacrament of Baptism is considered the "Door to the Church" and also a special Sacrament of initiation. You are becoming part of the Church and a baby is becoming part of the Family of the Church. The baby will become part of the "Church Militant" here on earth through the Sacrament of Baptism.

First thing to consider is choosing a baptismal date. In the Latin Mass, many parents will have an idea of the baby's due date and contact the church or chapel when the baby is born, so that the baptism can be arranged within the first week or so after birth. However, some Mexican cultural traditions wait and have the baptism a month or two after birth in order to have the whole family at the church during the baptismal ceremony. In fact, most likely you attend a regular

Novus Ordo – English Mass and most of those baptisms will be a month after birth. No matter what date the baptism is set for, this is a special day for the baby and family. Remember to have a fun celebration that day!

Next, one should take care to choose good godparents for the baby. After all the godparents should be someone you would trust to take care of your child if something ever bad happened to you, and you were killed or died. So, that's how we have chosen our godparents. Also, the godparents need to be practicing Catholic. And by practicing, we mean someone who attends Mass on a weekly basis and goes to the Sacraments like Confession and Holy Communion often. It does not help to choose a godparent who does not practice their faith. God parents do not have to be related – so you may choose a different godmother and godfather that are not related to each other – though it does make more sense to choose godmother and godfather that are husband and wife and friends of the family. This is just in case you choose an aunt or uncle and someone else like an older sibling!

Now, the "big day" is here – what rite will your child be baptized in and why? The Latin Traditional Rite of baptism still includes the minor exorcism and salt on the baby's tongue. The ceremony is a little bit longer and usually starts in the church vestibule and then proceeds into the church's baptistry area. Remember the godparents are the one's holding the baby – so you may want to diaper change the baby and feed baby before ceremony if possible. Only one of my children slept through the whole ceremony – I couldn't believe it. LOL. The other ones did not like the water and really cried a lot.

After the ceremony, the baby is usually presented to the front of Mary statue and consecrated to Our Lady with a short ceremony. Also, usually in the Latin Rite the priest sings the Salve Regina at the end of ceremony. Now, celebrate your newly baptized baby – doesn't that chrism oil smell so good?!! Have some cake and some people may give you gifts at this time as well!

Journal about Baptism and Churching of Women below:

Bonus C: Extra Saints of Pregnancy and Miscarriage/Stillbirth:

I have saints of motherhood in my postpartum book, and some do overlap! I also wrote about a few saints within the text area of this book. So, this section I am going to concentrate on saints that help with miscarriage/stillbirth and pregnancy as well.

My first thought is that many mother miscarry and have no one to pray to about this? I have found some saints of miscarriage that you may want to pray to help you "keep" this current pregnancy or to "help you get pregnant again".

There are two saint Catherine's that I have come across that have prayers for miscarriage recovery. There is not much known about St. Catherine of Siena being patroness of miscarriage – so I will share the prayer below. She is a third order Dominican and has other patronages as we discussed earlier in this book.

St. Catherine of Sweden is the other "Catherine", and she was the daughter of St. Bridget of Sweden. It is said that St. Bridget taught her daughter to pray for mothers who miscarried, and Catherine took on this task more after her mother's death. St. Catherine was married but lived as a "virgin" during her marriage -so they did not have any children. After her husband's death, she decided not to remarry and joined a religious order.

PRAYER TO ST. CATHERINE OF SWEDEN FOR HEALING AND CONSOLATION AFTER MISCARRIAGE[xciii]

Dear Saint Catherine, patron of those who have suffered a miscarriage, you know the dangers that await unborn infants. Please intercede for me that I may receive healing from the loss I have suffered. My soul has been deprived of peace and I have forgotten what true happiness is.

As I mourn the loss of my child, I place myself in the hands of God and ask for strength to accept His will in all things, for consolation in my grief, and for peace in my sorrow. Glorious Saint Catherine, hear my prayers and ask that God, in good time, grant me a healthy baby who will become a true child of God. Amen.

PRAYER TO ST. CATHERINE OF SWEDEN FOR A HEALTHY PREGNANCY AND FOR AVOIDING MISCARRIAGE[xciv]

Dear Saint Catherine, you know the temptations of mothers today as well as the dangers that await unborn infants. Intercede for me that I may avoid miscarriage and bring forth a healthy baby who will become a true child of God. Dear Heavenly Father, I thank and praise You for the gift of all human life. I am most especially grateful for the new life within my womb – the unborn child forming deep within me. Through the prayers of Mary, Mother of Jesus, and the intercession of Saint Catherine of Sweden, I beg You to watch over and protect this little one inside my womb.

In Jesus' Name. Amen.

I found another person named <u>Bl. Catalina</u> who is also a patroness of miscarriage and <u>stillbirth</u> and here's her story:

Bl. Catalina de María Rodríguez de Zavalía (1823-1896) was born Saturnina Rodríguez. She discerned a vocation to apostolic religious life when she was 17, but found that there were no apostolic women's religious communities in Argentina. Rather than encouraging her to found a new community or to leave the country to follow her vocation, Saturnina's spiritual director insisted that she get married to his (emotionally unstable and abusive) childhood friend Manuel, and become stepmother to Manuel's son and daughter. Though a loving stepmother, Saturnina struggled with infertility. She and Manuel had only one child in their 13 years of marriage, a daughter named Catalina who was stillborn. When Saturnina was 42, her husband died and she was able to follow her call to religious life. Despite seven years of opposition and setbacks, she persisted, and finally succeeded in establishing the community she had hoped to join more than 30 years earlier. When she made vows, she took the name Catalina de María, after her stillborn daughter Catalina. Mother Catalina spent the rest of her life as a spiritual mother to the many women who joined her order and the many people they served, including prostitutes, women of mixed race, poor women, and enslaved women.[xcv]

There's another "saint" or "blessed" this time a man who's wife suffered miscarriages – read about him below:

Bl. Frédéric Ozanam (1813-1853) is best known as the founder of the Society of St. Vincent de Paul, an international organization that provides direct personal service to the poor. He founded the Society at the age of 20 in response to an atheist friend who found evidence of the Church's charitable works of the past uncompelling. "What is your Church doing now?" he asked. "What is she doing for the poor of Paris? Show us your works and we will believe you!" Together with some of his friends, Frédéric did just that. While leading the Society, he was admitted to the Bar, earned a doctorate with a thesis on Dante, and became a professor of foreign literature. He married at 28 and doted on his wife Amélie, bringing her flowers on the

23rd of each month to commemorate their marriage. Together, they experienced the anguish of losing their first two children to miscarriage. After their first loss, they spent some time apart as Amélie attempted to recover at her parents' home; Frédéric wrote her almost daily until he was able to rejoin her. His beautiful letters speak of his sorrow, his longing for his wife, and the consolation he found in the Eucharist. The couple ultimately had a daughter, Marie, on whom Frédéric doted until his death from consumption at only 40.[xcvi]

Also, St. Gianna Molla is considered patroness of children and pregnancy – since I cover her in my motherhood section of the postpartum book – please read there about her!

Saint Zélie Martin is also patroness of miscarriage and pregnancy quote:

The little I did know about her revolved around her more famous daughter, St. Therese of Lisieux. But in addition to the Little Flower, Zélie was the mother to eight other children. Five of her daughters grew up to become religious sisters, but Zélie and her husband Louis also grieved the loss of four children. Three of their children passed away within their first year on earth, and they lost another at age five. Although losing children to miscarriage or an early death was a common experience in the 1800s, the honor and dignity that the Martins gave their children is inspiring.

The Martins often mentioned their children in Heaven during conversation with their living daughters. Even though they passed away before she was born, Therese wrote that her older siblings' intercession was part of her vocation story and her own journey to Heaven. Shortly after the canonization of Louis and Zélie, an icon was commissioned of the first married couple to be named saints together in modern times. The icon depicts all nine of the Martin children, emphasizing the dignity that Louis and Zélie strove to give every one of their children that God had blessed them with.

After Zélie's sister-in-law also experienced a miscarriage, Zélie reached out to her through a letter. "When I had to close the eyes of my dear children and bury them, I felt deep sorrow, but I was always resigned to it," she wrote. "I did not regret the pains and the sorrows which I had endured for them. Many persons said to me: 'It would have been better for you if you had never had them.' I could not bear that kind of talk. I do not think that the sorrows and the troubles endured could possibly be compared with the eternal happiness of my children with God. Besides, they are not lost to me forever; life is short and filled with crosses, and we shall find them again in Heaven. Above all, it was on the death of my first child that I felt more deeply the happiness of having a child in Heaven, for God showed me in a noticeable way that He accepted my sacrifice. Through the intercession of my little angel, I received a very extraordinary grace."[xcvii]

There are a few more saints of pregnancy, but I want to wrap up this little book. If you want to look up St. Margaret of Antioch – she battled a dragon (or devil) and it was like she was swallowed up by this dragon and spat out just like being birthed! So, pray to St. Margaret of Antioch if you are having a difficult birth!

St. Anne, St. Elizabeth, and Our Lady are all good patrons to pray to for pregnancy and birth! Read more about them in my postpartum book.

One last man saint: St. Raymond Nonnatus was born as a C-section baby! Back then this was a dangerous operation – however, his mother most likely died during the procedure – but he was cut out of her womb in order to save him. His name means "not born" since he did not come out the natural way![xcviii] His feast day is August 31st – so if you are having an August baby boy – this might be a good patron for your baby!

One final link – this is a link to a prayer ceremony for a mother who had a miscarriage – I just found this online and hope it will help another mother:

https://www.usccb.org/prayers/blessing-parents-after-miscarriage-or-stillbirth

Doula Resources:

Catholic Doula Program: http://catholicdoula.com

Other Books to consider reading:

Made For This by Mary Haseltine

A Catholic Postpartum by Julie Larsen – look for the newest version called second edition or has a rose on first – but they are all good!

Christian Childbirth

Christian Childbirth Handbook

Christ Centered Childbirth

Bibliography:

---

[i] https://kidadl.com/articles/st-therese-of-lisieux-quotes-from-the-little-flower-of-jesus
[ii] https://dowym.com/voices/inspiring-quotes-from-st-therese-of-lisieux/
[iii] https://everydaypower.com/st-therese-of-lisieux-quotes/
[iv] https://everydaypower.com/st-therese-of-lisieux-quotes/
[v] https://www.mamanatural.com/how-to-swaddle-a-baby/
[vi] This Photo by Unknown Author is licensed under CC BY-NC-ND
[vii] https://www.mamanatural.com/how-to-swaddle-a-baby/
[viii] This Photo by Unknown Author is licensed under CC BY-ND St. Gerard
[ix] https://www.mamanatural.com/how-to-swaddle-a-baby/
[x] This Photo by Unknown Author is licensed under CC BY-SA St. Joseph
[xi] https://www.ourcatholicprayers.com/prayers-to-st-gerard.html
[xii] https://www.daily-prayers.org/angels-and-saints/prayers-to-saint-gerard-majella/
[xiii] https://www.ewtn.com/catholicism/devotions/prayer-for-st-josephs-protection-329
[xiv] "Holiness consists simply in doing God's will, and being just what God wants us to be." – St Therese of Lisieux https://everydaypower.com/st-therese-of-lisieux-quotes/
[xv] https://www.pampers.com/en-us/pregnancy/pregnancy-calendar/10-weeks-pregnant
[xvi] https://www.parents.com/pregnancy/week-by-week/11/
[xvii] https://www.babycenter.com/pregnancy/week-by-week/10-weeks-pregnant
[xviii] https://www.babycenter.com/pregnancy/week-by-week/10-weeks-pregnant
[xix] Same as above.
[xx] https://www.babycenter.com/pregnancy/week-by-week/11-weeks-pregnant
[xxi] https://americanpregnancy.org/healthy-pregnancy/pregnancy-complications/hyperemesis-gravidarum-880/
[xxii] Same as above.
[xxiii] Same as above.

xxiv St. Therese's Autobiography

xxv St. Anne picture creative commons.

xxvi https://kidadl.com/articles/st-therese-of-lisieux-quotes-from-the-little-flower-of-jesus

xxvii https://www.bluearmy.com/the-little-way-of-st-therese-through-mary-to-jesus/

xxviii https://americanpregnancy.org/healthy-pregnancy/week-by-week/12-weeks-pregnant-1285/

xxix https://www.babycenter.com/pregnancy/week-by-week/12-weeks-pregnant

xxx https://parenting.firstcry.com/articles/12-weeks-pregnant-with-twins-or-multiples/

xxxi This Photo by Unknown Author is licensed under CC BY-NC-ND plum picture

xxxii https://www.pampers.com/en-us/pregnancy/pregnancy-calendar/13-weeks-pregnant

xxxiii Same as above – quote from website.

xxxiv https://www.pampers.com/en-us/pregnancy/multiple-pregnancy/article/twin-pregnancy-week-by-week

xxxv Creative commons picture nursing.

xxxvi http://www.mycatholicblog.com/st-emilia-the-mother-of-five-saints/

xxxvii https://kidadl.com/articles/st-therese-of-lisieux-quotes-from-the-little-flower-of-jesus

xxxviii https://www.verywellfamily.com/14-weeks-pregnant-4158944

xxxix https://www.babycenter.com/pregnancy/week-by-week/15-weeks-pregnant

xl Creative commons picture

xli https://eibalance.com/2013/03/03/anorexia-through-the-ages-from-sainthood-to-psychiatry/

xlii https://eibalance.com/2013/03/03/anorexia-through-the-ages-from-sainthood-to-psychiatry/

xliii https://www.eatingdisorderhope.com/blog/fasting-history-anorexia-nervosa

xliv This Photo by Unknown Author is licensed under CC BY-NC-ND

xlv https://www.tfp.org/26-quotes-by-saint-therese-of-lisieux-to-inspire-you/

xlvi https://www.whattoexpect.com/pregnancy/week-by-week/week-16.aspx

xlvii https://flo.health/pregnancy/week-by-week/17-weeks-pregnant

xlviii https://flo.health/pregnancy/week-by-week/17-weeks-pregnant

xlix https://www.thebump.com/a/essential-oils-for-pregnancy-basics#3

l This Photo by Unknown Author is licensed under CC BY-NC-ND

li http://www.romancatholicidentity.com/2010/02/st-agatha-patron-saint-of-breast-cancer.html

lii This Photo by Unknown Author is licensed under CC BY-SA St. Agatha (I guess numbering system starts over again).

liii This Photo by Unknown Author is licensed under CC BY-NC-ND (St Therese and roses picture)

liv This Photo by Unknown Author is licensed under CC BY-SA-NC

lv https://sspx.org/en/i-am-your-mother-lady-of-guadalupe

lvi Same as above link – quote from article above.

lvii This Photo by Unknown Author is licensed under CC BY-NC-ND (Guadalupe)

lviii Same as above picture

lix https://americaneedsfatima.org/Our-Blessed-Mother/protectress-of-the-unborn-our-lady-of-guadalupe.html

lx https://sancta.org/prayers.html

lxi https://www.coraevans.com/blog/article/10-most-powerful-st.-therese-of-lisieux-quotes

lxii This Photo by Unknown Author is licensed under CC BY-NC-ND

lxiii Same as above. (coraevans link)

lxiv https://www.pampers.com/en-us/pregnancy/pregnancy-calendar/20-weeks-pregnant

lxv Same as above (mom section).

lxvi https://www.pampers.com/en-us/pregnancy/pregnancy-calendar/21-weeks-pregnant

lxvii Same as above link…

lxviii https://thetuckerbunch.wordpress.com/2007/12/20/christian-modesty/

lxix http://www.traditionalcatholicpriest.com/2015/02/03/traditional-quotes-saints-modesty/

lxx Julie Larsen original prayer.

lxxi https://dowym.com/voices/inspiring-quotes-from-st-therese-of-lisieux/

lxxii https://everydaypower.com/st-therese-of-lisieux-quotes/

lxxiii https://diabetestalk.net/blood-sugar/why-are-babies-bigger-with-gestational-diabetes

lxxiv https://pubmed.ncbi.nlm.nih.gov/10561636/

lxxv http://consciouswoman.org/wp-content/uploads/gd-handout.pdf

lxxvi IBD (same as above link).

lxxvii This Photo by Unknown Author is licensed under CC BY-SA-NC

lxxviii https://aleteia.org/2016/07/08/once-we-met-saint-dymphna-everything-changed-for-the-good/

lxxix https://everydaypower.com/st-therese-of-lisieux-quotes/

lxxx March of Dimes Breastfeeding is licensed under CC BY-SA-NC

lxxxi kelly-sikkema-DPmevL6jcHo-unsplash.jpg

lxxxii https://everydaypower.com/st-therese-of-lisieux-quotes/

lxxxiii https://www.verywellhealth.com/bishop-score-5183938

lxxxiv https://www.verywellfamily.com/induction-labor-4013753

lxxxv Same as above.

lxxxvi www.catholicicing.com

lxxxvii garrett-jackson-oOnJWBMlb5A-unsplash.jpg picture credit

lxxxviii https://birthweeklynews.wordpress.com/2014/02/03/newborns-no-hatting-patting-chatting/

lxxxix https://www.pinterest.com/pin/209839663871217238/

xc This Photo by Unknown Author is licensed under CC BY-NC-ND

xci https://everydaypower.com/st-therese-of-lisieux-quotes/

xcii Unknown photo is licensed under CC BY-SA-NC

xciii https://www.tomakeamommy.com/praying-to-st-catherine-of-sweden-for-healing-and-protection-from-miscarriage/

xciv https://www.tomakeamommy.com/praying-to-st-catherine-of-sweden-for-healing-and-protection-from-miscarriage/

xcv https://catholicsay.com/saints-who-lost-a-child-to-miscarriage/

xcvi https://catholicsay.com/saints-who-lost-a-child-to-miscarriage/

xcvii https://aleteia.org/2018/08/20/3-women-saints-who-know-the-pain-of-miscarriage/2/

xcviii https://www.maryhaseltine.com/2018/10/some-patron-saints-for-pregnancy-and.html